CARING ENOUGH TO CONFRONT

The Love-Fight

David Augsburger

HERALD PRESS
Scottdale, Pennsylvania
Waterloo, Ontario

Scripture quotations in this publication are from the following versions:
Phillips—The New Testament in Modern English, Revised Edition, J.B. Phillips, Translator. © J.B. Phillips 1958, 1960, 1972. Used by permission of Macmillan Publishing Co. Inc.
NEB—The New English Bible. © The Delegates of the Oxford University Press and The Syndics of the Cambridge University Press 1961, 1970. Reprinted by permission.
NASB—New American Standard Bible. © The Lockman Foundation 1960, 1962, 1963, 1968, 1971, 1972, 1973, 1975. Used by permission.

Do you know . . .
- *how to deal with anger?*
- *how to experience the freedom of change?*
- *how to venture out in faith?*
- *how to cope with blame and prejudice?*
- *how to build trust?*

Caring Enough to Confront *describes the art of peacemaking. This completely revised and updated edition continues to be one of the best resources on "how to get along with people." And that's something we all need to know and do!*

Contents

Preface
To Revised Edition

"Creative living is care-fronting in conflict," I wrote to preface this manuscript in the spring of 1973. Now, seven years later in 1980, I find it even more true.

When my thrust as a person—my hopes, dreams, wants, needs, drives—runs counter to your thrust, there is conflict. To sacrifice my thrust is to be untrue to the push and pull of God within me. To negate your thrust is to refuse to be reverent before the presence and work of God within you.

Caring, confronting and integrating your needs and wants with my needs and wants in our joint effort toward creating Christian community is what effective living is about.

It is not the conflicts that need to concern us, but how the conflicts are handled. The frontal impact of our coming together can be creative, strengthening, and growth producing. This concern for a balanced wholeness of personal integrity, and sensitivity to persons runs throughout these essays on care-fronting as a creative way of uniting care and candor in life's relationships.

The teachers, colleagues, friends who contributed to this are many. Frank Kimper, Jan and Myron Chartier and the consultants in both the radio and print releases which originated the original manuscript—Roy Umble, Dan Heinrichs, Jim Gaede, Ernie Isaacs, Ken Weaver, Waldo Neufeld, Jim Fairfield, Matt Meyer.

After 10 printings, a revision and enlargement has been made. A chapter on confrontation is added. Sections on basic skills in listening, in trusting, in appreciating and expressing anger, in understanding prejudice, and in facilitating change in self and others have been strengthened.

It is New Year, 1980, as this revision is completed. To Nancy and to me, reviewing and revising a book on caring and confrontation which has come from and contributed to our relationship reminds us again that wholeness begins in the meeting of grace and truth, love and power.

David Augsburger

I love you.

If I love you
I must tell you
the truth.

I want your love.

I want your truth.

Love me enough to
tell me the truth.

1
Care-fronting:

The Creative Way Through Conflict

A good word: Caring. A bad word: Confronting.

Together they provide the balance of love and power which lead to effective human relationships.

The more common practice is to keep these distinct and separate.

"There is a time for caring.

"There is a time for confronting.

"Each in its own time. Care when caring is called for, confront when confrontation is required.

"Each in its own right. Caring dare not be contradicted by any mixture of confrontation. And confronting must not be contaminated by any admixture of caring. Each weakens the other. To confront powerfully, lay care aside. To care genuinely, candor and confrontation must be forgotten, for the moment at least.

"When I'm angry, I confront. To talk of caring at a moment like that would be false. When I care deeply about another, I cannot confront because hurting another is the very last thing I want.''

A third word: Care-fronting. A good word.

Care-fronting is offering genuine caring that bids another grow. (To care is to welcome, invite and support growth in another.)

Care-fronting is offering real confrontation that calls out new insight and understanding. (To confront effectively is to offer the maximum of useful information with the minimum of threat and stress.)

Care-fronting unites love and power. Care-fronting unifies concern for relationship with concerns for goals. So one can have something to stand for (goals) as well as someone to stand with (relationship) without sacrificing one for the other, or collapsing one into another. Thus one can love powerfully and be powerfully loving. These are not contradictory. They are complementary.

"That was a tasteless thing to do, just like your mother. . ." your husband mutters over dinner. You swallow twice at food gone flat, freeze into angry silence, get up from the table. (Familiar routine. He cuts. You retreat to lick the wound.)

You see in his eyes that he knows your next move— retreat to the bedroom, an evening and night of cold, withdrawn anger. When you feel rejected, you reject. (So? He cuts you off, off you go to sulk.)

"What's the point in running?" you ask yourself. "The longer I brood, the more I hurt. One of these times I'll tell him just how I feel." (Good! Say what you feel, say what you want, say where you are!)

Now is the time, you decide. Your feelings rush out. "When you criticize me like that, I feel rejected. I hurt. I usually run. But what I really want is to get around the wall between us and be able to feel close to you again. And I want you to respect me as me. I am not my mother. I am who am." He's looking surprised. He's not used to hearing you describe your feelings so clearly. He's seldom heard you say what you really want.

(When cut by another's sharp words, you decide, silent withdrawal is self-defeating. What matters most is getting in touch again. I can confront by saying what I really want. I care enough to say what I really feel.)

Care-fronting is the way to communicate with both impact and respect, with truth and love.

"Speaking the truth in love" is *the way* to mature right relationships.

Care-fronting has a unique view of conflict. Conflict is natural, normal, neutral, and sometimes even delightful. It can turn into painful or disastrous ends, but it doesn't need to. Conflict is neither good nor bad, right nor wrong. Conflict simply is. How we view, approach and work through our differences does—to a large extent—determine our whole life pattern. There are multiple views.

I might view conflict as *a given,* as a fixed matter of fate, explaining, "We just can't get along—we're incompatible— we'll never understand each other—that's all there is to it," then my life pattern would be one of avoiding threat and going my own safe, secure, well-armored way.

I could see conflict as *crushing,* "If we clash, I'll be judged—I'll be rejected—our friendship will fall through," then my life pattern would be acting the nice guy, quickly giving in to keep things comfortable.

I could view conflict as *an inevitable issue* of right and wrong, "I owe it to you, to me, to others, to God, to defend my truth and show you your error." Then my life would be rigid, perhaps perfectionistic, and judgmental.

I might begin to see conflict as *a mutual difference* to be resolved by meeting each other half way. "I'll come part

ay. Let's cooperate, compromise or put
ome joint way." Then my life pattern
g, meet-me-in-the-middle style of one-for-
for-you cooperation.

n come to see conflict as *natural, neutral, normal.* I
ay then be able to see the difficulties we experience as
tensions in relationships and honest differences in perspective
that can be worked through by caring about each other and
each confronting the other with truth expressed by love.

Each of these life patterns, or a combination of two, three
or four of the five, characterizes the conflict styles of most
adults in your life. If you have them in the order listed, you
are frequently frustrated, misunderstood, alienated or just
painfully confused about yourself and others. If your views
are in reverse order, you're already chuckling and feeling
good about the skills you either inherited or learned for
resolving conflict. New skills can be learned. You'll add at
least one by the end of this chapter.

"He's stealing me blind," you say, numb with anger.
"Over $300 must have come in across the counter today, and
his cash register ticket shows $175.

"Of all the stupid blunders, going into a partnership with
my brother-in-law has got to be the all-time winner," you
say. Opening your pharmacy together had seemed so right.
But in the first nine months you've barely turned a profit.

"The rat. He's been pocketing the cash, ringing up no-
sales, or avoiding the register altogether." Whatever the
system, he's picking you clean.

"I'll get him. I'll fix his wagon good, the embezzler."
Oh, but you can't. It'll hurt your sister more than him, and
she's just pulling away from a long depression.

"I'll shut up and get out. He can buy my half and have the
whole thing—debt, mortgage and all—right in his inadequate
lap." Not so easy. Your home was mortgaged too for the

operating capital. You're in all the way. To get out, you'll have to let him know you know.

"I'll give in and just sit on it for the time being. I'll wait for the auditor to catch it, or for him to hang himself by getting even more greedy. (Maybe if I give him a bonus, or commend him more for his work it will make him unbearably guilty.)

"I'll go halfway, I'll go along with him for a while, not say a thing, just stick so close he'll have to play fair." But breathing down his neck as you peer over his shoulder is a temporary compromise solution. You can't be there all the time.

"I've got to confront him with the goods. There's no other way out of the mess. But how do I do it?"

The five options: (1) I'll get him, (2) I'll get out, (3) I'll give in, (4) I'll meet you halfway, or (5) I care enough to confront, are the basic alternatives open in most conflict situations.

1. *"I'll get him"* is the I-win-you-lose-because-I'm-right-you're-wrong position in conflict. From this viewpoint, the attitude toward conflict is that the issues are all quite clear—and simple. Someone is right—totally right, and someone is wrong—completely wrong. Fortunately, I'm right (as usual) and you're wrong. (Except, in this case, it could prove to be someone else besides or instead of truth—on my side. It's my duty to put you right. This "win-lose" stance uses all power and little or no love. Goal is valued above relationship. "My way is the only way," the person feels.

2. *"I'll get out"* is the I'm-uncomfortable-so-I'll-withdraw stance toward conflict. The viewpoint here is that conflicts are hopeless, people cannot be changed; we either overlook them or withdraw. Conflicts are to be avoided at all costs. When they threaten, get out of their way.

Withdrawal has its advantages if instant safety is the all-important thing. But it is a way out of conflict, not a way through. And a way out is no way at all.

In this lose-lose stance everyone loses. There is no risk of power, no trusting love. "Show me to the nearest exit," the person requests over the shoulder. It's a no-way or any way response of flight.

3. *"I'll give in"* is the I'll-yield-to-be-nice-since-I-need-your-friendship approach. This perspective on conflict says that differences are disastrous. If they come out into the open, anything can happen. Anything evil, that is. It's far better to be nice, to submit, to go along with the other's demands and stay friends.

Yielding to keep contact will serve you well in many situations. But as a rule, it falls short. You become a doormat. A nice guy or gal. Frustrated. Yet smiling. The more tense and tight on the inside, the more generous and submissive on the outside.

4. *"I'll meet you halfway"* is the I-have-only-half-the-truth-and-I-need-your-half position. The attitude is one of creative compromise. Conflict is natural, and everyone should be willing to come part way in an attempt to resolve things. A willingness to give a little will lead to a working solution which is satisfactory to everyone.

Compromise is a gift to human relationships. We move forward on the basis of thoughtful, careful consensus and compromise in most decisions in conflict. But it calls for at least a partial sacrifice of deeply held views and goals which may cost all of us the loss of the best to reach the good of agreement.

When we begin with a decision to compromise, we run the risk that my half of the truth added to your half may not give us the whole truth and nothing but the truth. We may have two half-truths. Or the combination may produce a whole untruth. Only when we care enough to tussle with truth can we test, retest, refine and perhaps find more of it through our working at it seriously.

5. *"I care enough to confront"* is the I-want-relationship-and-I-also-want-honest-integrity position. Conflict is viewed as neutral (neither good nor bad) and natural (neither to be avoided nor short-circuited). Working through differences by giving clear messages of "I care" and "I want," which both care and confront, is most helpful.

This is interpersonal communication at its best. Caring—I want to stay in respectful relationships with you, *and* confronting—I want you to know where I stand and what I'm feeling, needing, valuing and wanting.

Caring	*Confronting*
I care about our relationship.	I feel deeply about the issue at stake.
I want to hear your view.	I want to clearly express mine.
I want to respect your insights.	I want respect for mine.
I trust you to be able to handle my honest feelings.	I want you to trust me with yours.
I promise to stay with the discussion until we've reached an understanding.	I want you to keep working with me until we've reached a new understanding.
I will not trick, pressure, manipulate, or distort the differences.	I want your unpressured, clear, honest view of our differences.
I give you my loving, honest respect.	I want your caring-confronting response.

To visualize the interrelationship of caring and confronting, of love and power, of concern about relationships and concern for goals, the diagram (figure 1) places these two values on the scale of one to nine. This offers four quadrants and a center point of cooperation/compromise.

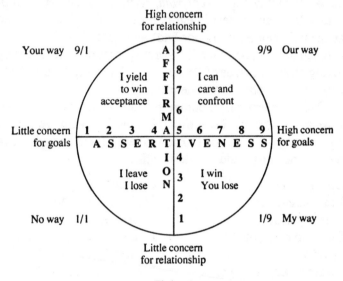

Figure 1

The "I-leave-I-lose" quadrant has little commitment to being either assertive or affirmative (thus measured on the one-to-nine scales it is called a 1/1 stance).

The "I-yield-to-win-acceptance" quadrant shows high commitment to maintaining or deepening relationships of approval but little to expressing a personal commitment to any threatening goal (thus it is high on affirmation, but is non-assertive in a 1/9 stance).

The "I-win-you-lose" quadrant is all assertiveness, often pure aggressiveness with little affirmation of the personal elements which prize relationships (thus 9/1).

The center of the diagram is the cooperative or compromising "Let's-each-come-halfway, meet-me-in-the-middle" stance (thus 5/5).

The "I-can-care-and-confront" quadrant is the caring

and confronting stance which places high value on both personal relationships and personal goals by seeking to create mutual relationships which work out joint goals (thus 9/9).

Each of these responses has its place in life. Each style of behavior has its appropriate time, situation and use.

The most effective usages are to begin insistently by (1) caring and confronting. If this is not effective in calling out a joint effort at reaching a mutually satisfactory solution, then (2) movement to a cooperative-compromise stance is well advised. This is hopefully a temporary solution which will open the opportunity to move toward enhanced caring and increased candor. If this fails, (3) it is wise to move toward a yield-to-maintain-relationship stance. Not as an end state, but as an intermediate commitment to build relationship so that more effective conversations and negotiations may follow. Only if this is rejected is it wise to move to (4) a win-lose stance of affirming goals even at the cost of sacrificing relationships. The hope, even in taking this assertive stance, is that one will be able to clarify the situation sufficiently to return to an equally affirmative and assertive relationship. If all of these prove ineffective, last choice (5) is a leave-and-lose move of withdrawal. Regretfully, one respects the other's right to refuse, reject, or withdraw for a period of separate growth and discovery. Hopefully, the conflict is alleviated by this, but the story has not reached the end.

Of the five options in conflict situations—(1) I win—you lose, (2) I want out, I'll withdraw, (3) I'll give in for good relations, (4) I'll meet you halfway, (5) I can care and confront—the last is the most effective, the most truly loving, the most growth-promoting for human relationships. But often it will be not the starting point but the long term goal.

When another comes on all "I win—you lose," it may be appropriate to respond with an "I'll give in for good relations" until the immediate storm is past. Then you can move back to an "I can care and confront" discussion

When another responds immediately with an "I want out—I withdraw" attitude, choosing to work toward a compromise or a temporary focus on relationships can be appropriate for the moment to affirm your deep interest in continuing friendship.

But moving back to care-confront openness as soon as possible is important to you both.

Rigid fixation in any one style or exaggerated dependence on any one behavior will seldom be effective. The ability to respond in varied ways and the flexibility to match one's response to the shape a conflict is taking, are crucial skills to be added to year by year.

As a model of the ability to respond genuinely and appropriately with both love and power in balance, two millennia of Christians have looked to the confrontive, caring and creative relationships modeled by Jesus of Nazareth. When examining His responses to various situations by using the language of conflict styles, one is immediately struck by His willingness to use any and all of the five as appropriate to His goals of redemptive compassion.

When the less-than-friendly hometown people of Nazareth rejected His message of confronting love, He chose to withdraw (see Luke 4:14-30). He cut off conversation and debate with the Pharisees when the point of clear rejection had arrived (see John 11:45-57).

Jesus was also free to act in an "I win—you lose" manner when this was the way to clearest understanding. He confronted the hucksters and hustlers in the Temple on win-lose terms (see Mark 11:11-19). Or read His clear statements to the religious leaders in Matthew 23, given after they had willed and arranged for His death.

At His arrest, during His interrogation, throughout His trial, in His unjust beating, and even through His execution,

Jesus chose to submit to the anger of others, absorb it, and speak back the word of forgiveness, grace and acceptance.

But no one has cared—and confronted—with greater effectiveness or more simple clarity than did Jesus.

To the would-be executioners of an accused adulteress, Jesus listened, waiting to hear their persistent questioning, to record all charges in the dust. *Caring.* Then He said, "Let the one among you who has never sinned throw the first stone at her." *Confrontation.*

To the woman, He said, " 'Where are they all—did no one condemn you?'. . .'No one, sir,' 'Neither do I condemn you.' " *Warm, understandable care.* "Go away now and do not sin again." *Clear, unmistakable confrontation* (John 8:7,10,11, *Phillips*).

To the rich, vain, conceited young ruler, Jesus listened, responded clearly, then looked at him and loved him. Then Jesus confronted. "Go, sell all, give to the poor; and come follow me." Clear enough (see Mark 10).

To Nicodemus (see John 3), to the outcast minority-group woman at the public watering place (see John 4), to the mayor of Capernaum whose son is at the point of death (see John 4) Jesus cared and confronted. He spoke truth in love. He was truth. He was love.

In his letter to Christians at Ephesus, Paul described the nature of Christian maturity as modeled in Jesus' own integration of truth and love:

> So shall we all at last attain to the unity inherent in our faith and our knowledge of the Son of God— to mature manhood, measured by nothing less than the full stature of Christ. . . .Let us speak the truth in love; so shall we fully grow up into Christ (Eph. 4:13,15, *NEB*).

John summarized the presence of God among us in Jesus with these same words.

> So the Word became flesh; he came to dwell among us, and we saw his glory, . . .full of grace and truth (John 1:14 *NEB*).

Truth with love brings healing.
Truth told in love enables us to grow.
Truth in love produces change.

Truth and love are the two necessary ingredients for any relationship with integrity. Love—because all positive relationships begin with friendship, appreciation, respect. And truth—because no relationship of trust can long grow from dishonesty, deceit, betrayal; it springs up from the solid stuff of integrity.

"Confrontation plus caring brings growth just as judgment plus grace brings salvation," says Howard Clinebell, Jr., a well-known pastoral counselor.

These are the two arms of genuine relationship: Confrontation with truth; affirmation with love.

I grow most rapidly when supported with the arm of loving respect, then confronted with the arm of clear honesty. Confronting and caring stimulate growth.

This is how God relates to us. When we speak of God's relationship with man we have historically used other words.

Judgment and grace lead to salvation.

God's judgment—radical honesty about truth—confronts us with the demands of disciplined maturity.

God's grace—undeserved love—reaches out to accept and affirm us at the point we know ourselves to be unacceptable.

Judgment cuts, even kills. If God dealt with us only in judgment, who could stand? If God reached out to us only in love, it would be a cheap grace without integrity. Mere divine permissiveness. "Anything goes" as far as heaven is concerned. Not so!

Judgment blended with grace.

Confrontation matched with caring.

Truth spoken in love.

Honesty, truth, trust, and love. These all interlock and intertwine in the biblical statements on relationships.

> Love in all sincerity. . . .Care as much about each other as about yourselves (Rom. 12:9 ,16, *NEB*).
>
> Love keeps no score of wrongs; does not gloat over other men's sins, but delights in the truth. There is nothing love cannot face; there is no limit to its faith, its hope, and its endurance (1 Cor. 13:5-7, *NEB*).
>
> "Love your neighbor as yourself." But if you go on fighting one another, tooth and nail, all you can expect is mutual destruction (Gal. 5:14,15, *NEB*).
>
> No, let us speak the truth in love; so shall we fully grow up into Christ. . .Bonded and knit together by every constituent joint, the whole frame grows through the due activity of each part, and builds itself up in love (Eph. 4:15,16, *NEB*).

For Further Experience

1. Do a mental rehearsal of both caring and confronting in conflicts you experienced today or anticipate tomorrow. Place the other person in a chair in front of you and hold out your left hand saying, "I do care, I want to respect you, I want your respect." Alternate by reaching out with the right hand to say, "But I want you to know how I feel. I want to tell you where I am. I have this goal in our relationship." Work both sides of yourself. Become aware of which is more difficult. In which are you least practiced? Stay with it until feelings of caring and statements of goal both become clear.

2. Check back through your relationships of the past week. Fill in appropriate situations.

(1) I win, you lose stance:

(2) I want out, I withdraw attitude:

(3) I'll give in for good relations:

(4) I'll meet you halfway:

(5) I can care and confront:

Which was effective? Which was most comfortable? Which was used most frequently? Which do you want to use more often?

I want to hear you,
    see what you see,
    feel what you feel

I want to be heard.
    Hear me as I hear you,
    Listen, I'm listening to you.

So I will speak simply
    with clear word windows
    that let you see
    all the way in
    to where I live
        laugh
        and
        cry.

2
Truthing It:
A Simplified Speech Style

"It's been months since I really talked with my husband; we've grown so far apart," you say in numb realization. "He has his life; I have mine. We see each other often but we rarely meet."

Your husband's job demands long hours. He has no time to hear you. Your job takes a lot of you. You're too tired to reach out to him. Now there's not even the old noise level of conflicts.

"Five years without conversation," you say. "We need to reshufle our cue cards and deal each other a new hand. If I only had the courage to suggest that tonight, suggest we try to find out what each of us expects from the other now. If I could listen well enough to invite him to start talking. Or better, I could ask about his needs, find out what he's wanting from me. Then perhaps we could begin to hear each other without fear."

Good relationship is two-way communication. When one side of the conversation is lost the relationship is dying. To the degree that equal responsiveness is lost, to that extent the relationship ceases to exist.

To love another is to invite, support, protect that person's equal right to hear and be heard.

When I listen: I want to hear you. To hear deeply. To hear openly. To attend to what is said, how it is said, what feeling is conveyed, and what is wanted. I want to hear you with the inner ear that is attuned to the feelings, the joys, the hurts, the angers, the demands of another.

I want to hear *you,* by going beyond just hearing myself interpreting you. I am aware of two strong tendencies: (1) to "read in" my interpretations as I listen and miss what you are wanting to tell me; and (2) to "read out" and totally miss what I don't want to hear from you because it threatens, confronts, rejects, ignores me and my viewpoint.

I want to hear you accurately, so I'll need to check out what I hear at crucial points to be as certain as possible that my meanings match your meanings. I get an inkling of what your meanings are from your words, your tone of voice, your face, gestures, and body movements. But it is only an inkling. I must check it out at times by replaying what I heard for your approval, until you agree that you have been heard.

I want to hear deeply, clearly, accurately enough that I am able—to some real extent—to feel what you feel, hurt where you hurt, and want for you the freedom to be all you are becoming.

When I speak: I want to speak simply. To say what I mean in the clearest, shortest, frankest words I know. I want to reach out with my meanings to meet your meanings. (Communication is a meeting of meaning.) Knowing that meanings are in people, not in words, I want to be as clear and open about my meanings as I can. (Words don't mean. People mean.)

I want to speak personally. Since I can speak only from my experience, I want to say, "I think. . . ," "I feel. . . ," "I want. . . ," instead of "People think. . ." or "You get the feeling. . ." To declare my personal feelings and convictions calls for courage. There is no risk in saying, "Most people," "it seems," "sometimes feel," "to some extent. . ." I will risk; I will reveal my true self; I will be increasingly vulnerable to you by respecting your perceptions equally with my own.

I want to speak for myself, not for others. I will not say, "We think. . ." "they say. . ." "people feel. . ." or "it's often said. . ."

I will not try to speak for you. I will not say, "I think you think I think. . ." I will not try to second guess your feelings, thoughts, attitudes. I do not care for mind reading or mind readers. I want to listen as you speak to me, and respond.

I want to speak honestly. Truthing it is trusting others with my actual feelings and viewpoints. Avoiding honest statements of real feelings and viewpoints is often considered kindness, thoughtfulness, or generosity. More often it is the most cruel thing I can do to others. It is a kind of benevolent lying.

Selective honesty is not honesty at all. I find myself using it (1) to avoid real relationships with others when I'm too rushed or bushed to give them my time; (2) to avoid clear confrontation with others; (3) to manipulate situations or facts to protect myself or others. I don't like such defense systems, no matter how comfortable they may seem. I want to be truthful in all situations. I want to pay others the compliment of believing they can handle honest feelings. I want to put out what I feel, where I am, how I think.

I want to speak directly. I do not want to talk about people when it is possible to talk to them. Whatever I have to say to you, I want you to hear first from me.

I want to negotiate differences with others in clear, respectful, truthful ways of speaking and acting. I want conflict to call out the best in myself and others. I want both the truth as I see it and respect for the other to be clear in my responses, verbal and nonverbal.

When situations of conflict become difficult, I want to speak clearly, honestly, personally, directly, in simple statements. This provides the greatest impact with the least confusion or distortion. I may or may not be able to break through the conflict to understanding, but I can express both love and truth best by refusing the "whys" and the "it's your faults."

"It's okay, Honey, no problem," you say to your husband on the phone. It's the fourth night in a row he's chosen to work late and called you with last-minute apologies. It's not really okay with you, even though you keep saying it is. But that's always been your style. Be agreeable, give in to others, say everything's okay, bottle your feelings until finally you explode over some stupidly simple thing and say things you hate as soon as you hear them.

Always giving in is no good. Accumulating grievances is even less helpful. Dishonest statements to cover it all is even worse. And when the anger eruption comes, it's totally ineffectual.

"I've got to start dealing with things as they come up, not just postpone my feelings and let them simmer," you say. "Like that phone call right now. I could have said, 'No, it's not okay. I have special things planned. I am irritated at your being out the last three nights. I want to be with you tonight.' I could have said it straight and simply."

What stops you from leveling like that? You stop yourself. "It's not too late," you tell yourself, "I can still ring him back." You pick up the phone and begin dialing. I'll say, "I want to be with you tonight. Try to change things. Come home on time. . . ."

"I can keep short books with my feelings. Stay up-to-date. Find ways of reporting feelings as they occur. Experiment in saying both what I feel and what I really want. "I do care about you. I want to be close. I want more time together. I need to tell you when I'm angry. Love me enough to listen to me."

"It is certain that a relationship will be only as good as its communication. If you and I can honestly tell each other who we are, that is, what we think, judge, feel, value, love, honor and esteem, hate, fear, desire, hope for, believe in and are committed to, then and then only can each of us grow. Then and then alone can each of us be what he really is, say what he really thinks, tell what he really feels, express what he really loves. This is the real meaning of authenticity as a person: that my exterior truly reflects my interior. It means I can be honest in the communicaion of my person to others. And this I cannot do unless you help me. Unless you help me, I cannot grow or be happy or really come alive.

"I have to be free and able to say my thoughts to you—to tell you about my judgments and values, to expose to you my fears and frustrations, to admit to you my failures and shames, to share my triumphs—before I can really be sure what it is that I am and can become. I must be able to tell you who I am before I can know who I am. And I must know who I am before I can act truly, that is, in accordance with my true self."[1]

"Why do you always leave your things lying all over the house?" you ask.

"Why can't you pick up after yourselves?"

"Why don't you show a little interest in things?"

No one answers you. It's like your questions go unheard.

"Why can't I get a little cooperation?"

Your son looks up at you. "Why does everything you say begin with the word 'why'?" he asks.

"Why shouldn't it?" you snap.

"I don't know," he says, "but it feels like a trap. If we say why, you can shout us down, say our reasons are no good."

"What do you want me to say?" you ask. (First question without a "why.")

"Just tell us what you want," he replies. "Like I'm doing to you now. Don't bear-trap us. Just be honest with us."

To communicate a message, make a statement. To ask for a message, use a question. Simplicity in speech is to state what should be stated, ask what needs to be asked, and to refuse to confuse the two. When questions are used as concealed ways to make statements, or statements are made as concealed questions, nonconstructive confusion results.

The most frequently misused communication pattern is the question. Questions can be clever, coercive, or concealed ways of either offering opinions or manipulating others. Six of the most commonly used pseudo-questions are:

The leading question. "Don't you feel that. . .?"; "Wouldn't you rather . . .?" This limits or restricts the range of possible responses and leads the witness down the primrose path to make an admission or commitment that the questioner wishes, not what the responder wants. Q. "Don't you think that. . . ?" A: "No, I don't think that. . . If you think that, I invite you to say it by speaking for yourself."

The punishing question: "Why did you say (do, try) that?" This punishes by seeking to arouse conflicts in the other or define the other person in such a way that infers there is inconsistency, contradiction or dishonesty between intention and action. Q: "Why did you do such a. . . ?" A: "I'll tell you what I want."

The demanding question: "When are you going to do

something about. . . ?" This actually makes a demand or sneaks in a hidden command under the guise of an innocent request for innocuous information. Q: "When are you going to get started on . . . ?" A: "Tell me when you want it."

The dreaming question: "If you were in charge here, would you rather . . . ?" This asks for hypothetical answers. The function is to criticize, to call a point of view impractical or irrelevant but to do it as a harmless fantasy. Q: "If you had the say around here, wouldn't you . . . ?" A: "I'd like to work with what is, now."

The needling question: "What are you waiting for?" or "What did you mean by that?" This multi-level question has a multiple choice of meanings: (1) Tell your meaning again, I'm listening. (2) What are you implying about me? (3) How dare you say that to me? (4) Can't you speak simple English, you clod. (5) You're attacking me. The needling question has as many levels as the listener may choose and it has no one-level. No matter which level the listener chooses to answer the questioner can say, "You misunderstood me."

The setting-up question: "Didn't you once say that . . . ?" This maneuvers the other into a vulnerable position, ready for the hatchet. Q: "Isn't it true that you once . . . ?" A: "Ask me about the here and now, I'm present."

I can do with a lot fewer questions. Especially those beginning with "why." "Why" questions are most often covert ways of attempted control. I want to eliminate "why" from my relationships. I will ask "what" and "how." These offer all the information I need to know to relate effectively. "Why" questions, evaluates, judges motives and intentions. "What" or "how" deal with what is wanted in our relationship and how we can get it.

I want to give statements instead of asking questions. Those questions which are simple requests for clarification or further information are useful. But hit and run questions are double-talk. They are ways of making comments, criticisms, or attacks while avoiding the full responsibility for what is said. They are ways of giving multi-level messages that leave the listener with a multiple choice test with every interaction. These, I can do without.

Love gives up the concealed weapons called questions and makes clear statements like: I care about you. I need you. I want your help. I want your respect. Love is honestly open in conversation. Love sets no traps.

"Why did you take the car last night when you knew I'd be needing it?" your husband says to your son—to your son's indifferent back. He shrugs his shoulders as a reply. ":I want to know why you deliberately defy me."

"Man, I'm just doing my thing," your son replies. "You're free to do yours."

They're talking past each other again. Do you want to intervene? "I want to know why you try to spite me," your husband is saying. The boy's ignoring him. To answer is to walk into a bear trap. If he answers, his dad will say, "That's stupid." It's like a cycle of move and countermove that you do your best to avoid.

"Count me out of their fights," you say. But maybe you could referee. Get them to agree to some simple ground rules. Maybe they could learn to fight a little more fairly?

A few simple guidelines for cleaning up fights are: the person who has a complaint should make the first move to discuss it; one complaint to a session; no trapping questions, just clear statements. Try giving honest, clean "beefs" (sharply pointed complaints or criticisms) like, "The behavior you do is. . ."; "When you do it I feel. . ."; "What I really want is. . ." Have the other repeat the beef. Then respond with a clear yes, no, or compromise offer.

Simple rules—but they're the way of truthing it in love through conflict.

Clear communication is giving clean, simple yes and no responses.

"Whatever you have to say," Jesus counseled, "let your 'yes' be a plain 'yes' and your 'no' be a plain 'no'—anything more than this has a taint of evil" (Matt. 5:37, *Phillips*).

Love is giving clear yes's and no's.

"Sure, count me in. I'll be glad to help," you say into the telephone receiver. "I like working with boys. Coaching Little League sounds fun. Right, I'll be at the meeting." You turn from the phone to face your wife's questioning eyes.

"It's just Monday and Thursday nights," you explain. "It's important for the community. I can't say no."

"If we had a boy in Little League, it'd be different," your wife says. "But, Joe, you don't have the time."

"I can make time for it," you say. "I just can't say no to things that oughta be done."

"But when you accept that," your wife replies, "you're saying no to having time with me and our girls, you're saying no to having time for yourself."

"Yeah, you're right. I've already got the club on Tuesdays, night school Wednesdays, bowling on Fridays, not to mention all the extras."

"When do you start saying no?" your wife asks. "With no time together, we're becoming strangers. And what time we do have we spend on working out our differences. There's no time just to be together."

"I can't say no," you begin again.

"Won't say 'no,' " your wife corrects.

"Yeah, that's it. I'm afraid they'll quit asking me in on things if I cut out once. I don't want to be passed by. But I want time with my family too. Maybe I can say no. I think I will."

When I decide, I want to give clear 'yes-signals' or

"no-signals." Yes signals come easy. No signals often come hard. "No" is one of the hardest words to pronounce—face to face.

"I can't say no to the boss," a young man tried to explain to me last night. "I've got to do what he asks. It's the only way open to me. I have no choice." I doubt it.

"I can't say no to Ted, I just can't." The young wife who gave that excuse for indecision over a growing friendship with her employer can't say no because she won't say no.

To say "I can't" is seldom true. More often it's a way of avoiding responsibility for making a decision. "I won't say no," would be more accurate. "I refuse to take responsibility for myself and say no."

You can say no—if you will. You can say no if you've first said a bigger yes to time for your family, time for close relationships, time to be human, time for personhood, time for your true self.

Say yes to your values. Guard that yes with your calendar.

You feel the stiffness around your mouth as you walk away from the boss. You know you must have had your perma-smile pasted on. Funny, you weren't smiling inside. Now you're going to rush through lunch so you can run an errand for the guy at the next bench. "No bother at all," you insisted. But it is. . .

"I'm a nice guy," you say to yourself. "I'm just too nice to people. I smile, I say yes—yes—yes, and yet inside I feel tired. I wish they'd lean on somebody else for a change. When they ask for something, I say, 'Anything for a friend.' If they impose, I say, 'What's a friend for?' If they get angry, I say, 'Come on, let's be friends.'

"I'm an insufferably nice guy. Except inside. There I'm like anybody else. What I'd like is to be able to say no. What I want is to be free to choose for myself, to really be me."

Speak the truth, be truthful, act truly. As Jesus said, "Let your yes be a clear yes, and your no, no. Anything more has the taint of evil."

For Further Experience

1. Practice listening skills to learn new ways of hearing, feeling with, caring for others.

(1) Sit at eye level with a child. Let your own inner child come out and play with the little boy or girl who is talking to you. Listen with your eyes. Check out what you're hearing. Find some way to affirm his or her preciousness.

(2) Listen to a friend. Communicate love without putting it in words. Avoid asking any questions, prompting or completing his sentences.

(3) Listen to someone you rather dislike. Try to really hear him or her, for a change. Become aware of your own resistance to getting close. Extend some word of understanding, appreciation, or simple joy.

(4) Listen to God. With pencil in hand. Take notes on new awarenesses. Let your mind flow freely, but keep things open by being aware that He is communicating love to you.

2. Practice simple, clear, single-level speech.

(1) Drop all exaggeration or additional coloring of language for effect; use fewer adjectives.

(2) Refuse all pretenses—of knowing things you only guess, of being better informed or more certain of facts than you are.

(3) Live for a day without questions. If you need information, say "I'm wondering if. . ." or "I'm wanting to know. . ."

(4) Find fresh clear ways of saying yes and no without dishonesty. Instead of "I'm sorry but I can't," try "No, thank you. I'm wanting that time for my family."

I am not angry!
  (I'm just concerned.)

I don't get angry!
  (I just feel hurt.)

See? You made me angry!
  (It's all your fault.)

See? You burn me up!
  (It's you in the wrong.)

3
Owning Anger:

Let Both Your Faces Show

Your wife made a cutting remark two days ago, and still no apology. Your daughter didn't thank you for the little gift you bought her. Your son forgot to put the tools back in their place in your shop. And you're feeling angry at all of them, at everything!

Anger is a demand.

Like, "I demand an apology from you—an apology that suits me."

"I demand you show appreciation for my gifts—in a way that pleases me."

"I demand that you return my tools—perfectly—just the way I keep them."

That's the real thrust of anger. A demand that also demands others meet your demands.

Even though you seldom put the demands into words, they are there inside the feelings, energizing the resentment.

"What if I said what I feel, if I really made my demands

clear? Then I could either stick to them, or cancel them, laugh at them and forget them. . ."

Freedom from being dominated by anger begins by tracking down the demands made on others. Recognizing them, admitting them out loud speeds up the process of owning the anger. Then one has a choice: (1) to negotiate the demands that matter, or (2) to cancel the ones that don't.

Freedom comes as one is candid and open in facing the demands made on others. Wisdom comes as one is willing to cancel unfair demands. Maturity comes through freeing others to live and grow without the imposition of controlling demands.

> Underneath my feelings of anger
> —there are concealed expectations.
> (I may not yet be aware of them myself.)
> Inside my angry statements
> —there are hidden demands.
> (I may not yet be able to put them
> into words.)

Recognized or unrecognized, the demands are there. Anger is a demand. It may be a demand that you hear me. Or that you recognize my worth. Or that you see me as precious and worthy to be loved. Or that you respect me. Or let go of my arm. Or quit trying to take control of my life.

The demands emerge whenever I see you as rejecting me or foresee you as about to reject me as a person of worth.

Dr. Frank Kimper, a great teacher of pastoral care, writes of this: "You are precious simply because you are. You were born that way. *To see that, and to be grasped by the reality of it, is to love.*

"Experience seems to indicate that harmonious relations are possible *only when that attitude is maintained.* This universal law has been stated in many ways—by the Jews as a simple and direct command of God, 'Thou shalt love thy neighbor as thyself.' The clause, 'as thyself,' correctly implies that *love of self is innate.* Every person senses *instinctively* the priceless nature of his own being, and reacts *reflexively* to preserve it against any threat.

"More specifically, each of us is automatically 'defensive' in the face of perceived rejection. To be ignored as though I did not exist, or to be treated as though I were worthless, is repulsive. Instinctively, spontaneously I react to affirm the priceless nature of my own being by becoming angry and lashing back or, feeling very hurt, by withdrawing within some protective shell to safeguard as best I can the treasured 'me' I know I am.

"But my reaction to being ignored or rejected has also a second purpose: to demand by angry words or pouting that others recognize the preciousness of the self I am, and respond accordingly. Such demands fail because in making my demand I reject and ignore the very persons I want to love me; and once horns are locked in that way, the only solution is for one or the other of us (or both) to adopt an attitude of love—to see and affirm the other to be as precious as I am, *no matter what his performance.*

"I have never met a human being who did not have similar spiritual reflexes. Because to love one's self is a 'built-in reflex.' Each of us was created that way."[2]

Anger is a demand "that you recognize my worth." When I feel that another person is about to engulf or incorporate me (assuming ownership of me, taking me for granted, using me, absorbing me into his or her life-program), I feel angry.

Actually, I first feel anxious. "Anxiety is a sign that one's self-esteem, one's self-regard is endangered," as Harry Stack Sullivan expressed it.[3] When my freedom to be me is threatened, I become anxious, tense, ready for some action.

Escape? Anger? Or work out an agreement?

Escape may be neither possible nor practical. Agreement seems far away since I see you as ignoring my freedom, devaluing my worth, and attempting to use me. Anger is the most available option.

Anger is "the curse of interpersonal relations," Sullivan well said. A curse, because it is so instantly effective as a way of relieving anxiety. When a person flashes to anger, the anger clouds his recall of what just happened to spark the anger, confuses his awareness of what he is really demanding, and restricts his ability to work toward a new agreement.

But we chose—consciously or unconsciously—to become angry because:

"Anger is much more pleasant to experience than anxiety. The brute facts are that it is much more comfortable to feel angry than anxious. Admitting that neither is too delightful, there is everything in favor of anger. Anger often leaves one sort of worn out. . .and very often makes things worse in the long run, but there is a curious feeling of power when one is angry.[4]

Check the pattern: (1) I feel keen frustration in my relationship with another; (2) I see the other person as rejecting me—my worth, my needs, my freedom, my request; (3) I become suddenly and intensely anxious; (4) I blow away my anxiety with anger which confuses things even further; (5) I may then feel guilty for my behavior and resentful of the other's part in the painful experience.

Anxiety is the primary emotion. It signals that a threat is received, a danger is perceived, or a devaluation has been "subceived" (subconsciously received) in another's response to me.

Anger is a secondary emotion. It signals that demands are being expressed toward the source of pain, hurt, frustration.

If I own my anxiety and deal constructively with my demands, my anxious arousal and my angry appraisal of the situation can be used to renegotiate relationships until they are mutually satisfactory.

You're standing in the living room, looking out the window at your son's back. You're replaying the last moment's conversation. "How stupid can you get?" you'd said. "You blew it again like a no-good kid. That's what you are and you better shape up or you're shipping out."

There he goes, anger and rejection showing in the slump of his shoulders. "He blew it?" you ask yourself. "Well, I blew it even worse. I get angry, I attack him personally, I put him down, I chop away at his self-esteem. I'm getting nowhere. What else can we do? If I could just deal with what he's doing without attacking him. Maybe that would make a difference. I could try it."

When on the receiving end of another's anger, I want to hear the anger-messages the other gives to me and check out what I am picking up as a demand. Careful listening can discern what the other is demanding, clarify it in clear statements, and lead to clean confrontation. Then I have the choice of saying yes to the other's demands or saying no. I may feel angry in return, but I want to experience my anger with honest "I statements," not with explosive "you statements."

Explosive anger is powerless to effect change in relationships. It dissipates needed energies, stimulates increased negative feelings, irritates the other persons in the transaction and offers nothing but momentary discharge. Vented anger may ventilate feelings and provide instant though temporary release for tortured emotions, but it does little for relationships.

Clearly expressed anger is something different. Clear statements of anger feelings and angry demands can slice through emotional barriers or communications tangles and establish contact.

When angry, I want to give clear, simple "I messages." "You messages" are most often attacks, criticisms, devaluations of the other person, labels, or ways of fixing blame.

"I messages" are honest, clear, confessional. "I messages" own my anger, my responsibility, my demands without placing blame. Note the contrast between honest confession and distorted rejection.

I Messages	You Messages
I am angry.	You make me angry.
I feel rejected.	You're judging and rejecting me.
I don't like the wall between us.	You're building a wall between us.
I don't like blaming or being blamed.	You're blaming everything on me.
I want the freedom to say yes or no.	You're trying to run my life.
I want respectful friendship with you again.	You've got to respect me or you're not my friend.

Anger is a positive emotion, a self-affirming emotion which responds reflexively to the threat of rejection or devaluation with the messages (1) I am a person, a precious person and (2) I demand that you recognize and respect me.

The energies of anger can flow in self-affirming ways when directed by love—the awareness of the other person's equal preciousness.

Anger energies become a creative force when they are employed (1) to change my own behavior which ignored the other's preciousness and (2) to confront the other with his or her need to change unloving behavior. Anger energy can be directed at the cause of the anger to get at the demands I am making, to own them, and then either correct my demanding self by canceling the demand or call on the other to hear my demand and respond to how I see our relationship and what I want.

Focusing anger on the person's behavior frees one to stand with the other even as you stand up for your demands. The freedom to express appreciation for the other as a person, even as you explain your anger at his or her way of behaving, lets you stay in touch while getting at what you are angry about. You can be both angry (at behaviors) and loving (toward persons) at the same time.

Anger erupted in a place of worship, the synagogue.

A handicapped man with paralysis of the hand came asking Jesus for healing. The religious leaders are (1) looking on with malice, (2) anticipating that Jesus may break their ceremonial blue laws against doing a service for another on the Sabbath, (3) hoping for some such infraction of the law so they can charge Him with illegal, irreligious, irresponsible action.

Jesus avoids neither the man in need nor His own critics.

"Stand up and come out here in front," He says to the man.

Then He turns to the Pharisees. He is aware of their demands—demands characteristic of many religious leaders through the centuries—(1) that principles come before the pain of persons, (2) that religious piety be honored above the needs of a brother, (3) that legalistic obedience is more important than human life and love for others. Jesus focuses their demands in the kind of question-statements they were so fond of debating. "What is truly right, just, good? To do good or to do evil on the Sabbath? To save life or to destroy it?" But in acting so, He is clearly confronting and refusing their demands.

There is silence. (As an answer, silence is often violence.)

Jesus is deeply hurt at their inhumanity.

He looks at them in anger. His look sweeps from one face

to another. His demand is clear. Be human. Be loving. Care about people. Respect this man's needs. See him as precious.

Then Jesus does the responsible, loving, caring thing. "Stretch out your hand," He says to the man.

He stretches it out, and it is as sound as the other (Mark 3:1-6, paraphrased from *Phillips*).

That is clear, focused, creative, controlled, dynamic anger.

Hate is sin	Love is virtue
Anger is evil	Affection is good
Confronting is brutal	Caring is wonderful
Openness is questionable	Diplomacy is wise

Do you find yourself thinking in such clearly defined categories? Rejecting hate, anger, honest awareness, and expression of your true feelings and perspectives and clear confrontation with others? To cut off one-half of your emotional spectrum and reject all negative feelings is to refuse to be a whole person. To deny and repress everything on the negative side is to also stifle and crush the full expression of your positive side.

There is danger in abusing and misusing others with our positive emotions and actions—love, kindness, gentleness, tolerance, sweetness—just as there is the threat of cutting and destroying others with our negative responses—anger, harshness, criticism, irritation. To be engulfed and incorporated by a smothering love, all sweet gentleness, and I'm-only-trying-to-help-you-it's-for-your-own-good kindness is more treacherous than harsh, crisp frankness. You can at least reject frankness without fighting an affectionate sticky mass of divinity-candy love.

To be a whole person in relationships, risk sharing both sides of yourself. Be open with both your negatives (honest anger) and your positives (affirming love). Let both your faces show. There are two sides in everyone. Both sides are important. Both are acceptable. Both are precious. Both can be loved.

We prefer to think that God wants our very best and only our best; that God will have nothing to do with weakness, timidity, or fears.

Not so. God accepts weakness as well as strength, fear as well as confidence, anger as well as gentleness.

God loves whole persons.

Such love makes wholeness possible in its most complete form. As we know and experience the love of God, acceptance reaches out to include both sides of us. "God knows the best and worst about us; and what do you know? God loves us anyway."

I can be aware of my feelings of anger. (I am accepted.)

I can own my resentments, my hate, my hostility. (I am loved.)

I can discover new ways of experiencing my negative and my positive feelings. (I am free to grow.)

I can be angry in creative, loving, caring ways. (I see it modeled in Jesus.)

Harry's been your friend for years. You could always count on him. Now you hurt him. He's turned against you. Last month it was Steve. You cut him off in an angry moment; it hasn't been the same. People you've been close to for years now hold you at a distance.

"So what. If they want to let me down, who needs them," you tell yourself. But inside you say, "I need them. I want their friendship. But I drive them away from me. It's like I've been carrying an overload of anger in my gut.

"I've got to talk it out with someone," you tell yourself. But where do you turn? "I need to talk to someone about who to talk to," you say. "Maybe my minister would listen to me and suggest where I could find out what's bugging me."

(When you find yourself carrying an overload of anger as extra baggage, talk it out with someone you trust—a friend, your minister, your doctor. And reach out to others for new ways of respectful behaving that you get where you really want to be with your friends.)

"I just can't help it. It makes me angry."

"It just gets to me and touches off my temper."

"It's like something comes over me and I can't do a thing about it."

"It's other people, that's what it is. They know I've got a quick temper and they're out to get me."

"It" is the problem. "It" causes untold irritation, anger, frustration, embarrassment, pain, guilt, and misery. "It" is not me. "It" is this something, or someone, or some situation.

When you find yourself using "it" as an explanation or as a scapegoat, stop. Listen to yourself. Recognize what you're doing; avoiding responsibility; sidestepping the real problem; denying ownership of your feelings, responses, and actions.

Release comes not from denying but from owning who—what—and where I am in my relationships.

I want to own what goes on in me and accept total responsibility for it.

I discover that as I own it, accepting full responsibility, I am then able to respond in new ways. I become response-able.

A great freedom comes as I own my thoughts, feelings, words, and emotions: (1) I become free to choose my actions; (2) I become free to choose my reactions.

My actions are mine. Your actions are yours. I am responsible for my behavior. You are responsible for yours.

I also accept responsibility for my actions.

"You make me angry," I used to say.

Untrue. No one can make another angry. If I become angry at you I am responsible for that reaction. (I am not saying that anger is wrong. It may well be the most appropriate and loving response that I am aware of at that moment.)

But *you* do not make me angry. *I* make me angry at you. It is not the only behavior open to me.

There is no situation in which anger is the only possible response. If I become angry (and I may, it's acceptable) it's because I choose to respond with anger. I might have chosen kindness, irritation, humor, or many other alternatives (if I had been aware of these choices). There is no situation which commands us absolutely. For example, I have the choice to respond to another's threat with blind obedience, with silent passivity, with vocal refusal, with firm resistance, or with anger, if that seems appropriate.

When childhood experiences are limited, a person may mature with a limited set of behaviors open to him or her. Some have only two ways of coping with another's attack— anger or submission. If these are the only ways modeled by the parents or the family, they may be the only aware-choices in the person's behavioral repertoire.

If I have grown enough in life so that more than one pattern of behavior is available to me, then I can freely select the responses which seem most appropriate to the situation.

I want to be aware of a wealth of responses and to have them available to me. Anger or patience. Toughness or gentleness. Clear confrontation or warm, caring support. I want to be able-to-respond in any of these.

I am responsible for choosing my responses to you.

I am responsible for the way I react to you.

I am responsible for how I see you. And from the way I see you—as either friendly or hostile, accepting or rejecting, welcoming or threatening—emerge my feelings. Feelings are the energies that power the way I choose to see you or to perceive you.

I am responsible for how I see you—and from that for the way I feel about you.

You cannot make me angry. Unless I choose to be angry.

You cannot make me discouraged or disgusted or depressed. These are choices.

You cannot make me hate. I must choose to hate.

You cannot make me jealous. I must choose envy.

I experience all these and more on all too many occasions, but I am responsible for those actions or reactions. I make the choice.

And I am free to choose loving responses. I am free to choose trusting replies. I am free to react in concerned, understanding ways if I choose to see the other person as precious, as valuable, as worthy of love because he or she is equally loved of God.

I love me.	I also love you.

I love my freedom
   to be who I am.
	I respect your freedom
	   to be who you are.

I love my drive
   to be all I can be.
	I admire your drive
	   to be all you can be.

I love my right
   to be different from you.
	I recognize your right
	   to be different from me.

I love my need
   to be related to you.
	I appreciate your need
	   to be related to me.

The thoughts I think,
The words I speak,
The actions I take,
The emotions I feel—
   They are mine. For them
   I am fully responsible.
	The thoughts you think,
	The words you speak,
	The actions you take,
	The emotions you feel—
	   They are yours. For them
	   I am in no way
	   responsible.

I am free
to accept or to refuse
   your wants
	You are free
	to accept or to refuse
	   my wants

your requests
your expectations
your demands.
I can say yes.
I can say no.
I am not in this world
   to live as you prescribe.

I am not responsible
   for you.
I will not be
   responsible *to* you.
I want to be
   responsible *with* you.

my requests
my expectations
my demands.
You can say yes.
You can say no.
You are not in this world
   to live as I prescribe.

You are not responsible
   for me.
You need not be
   responsible *to* me.
You can be
   responsible *with* me.

For Further Experience

1. Read Psalm 40, and notice David's frank honesty with God as the feelings flow out. List the feelings from depression, to release, to elation, to fear, to joy in helping others, to anger, to resentment, to trust and final impatience.

2. To put your negative feelings into words and own them as a part of the you God loves, complete the phrases in at least five ways:

I get angry when:
And my behavior is:
And afterward I feel:
What I really want is:

3. To get in touch with the demands inside your anger, end this sentence in five ways:

When I become angry, my demands are:

4. To explore new behaviors in conflict situations, finish this line as a creative rehearsal of new ways of responding to others:

When I am angry, I want to try:

I differ from you.
   (To differ is not to reject.)

I disagree with you.
   (To disagree is not to attack.)

I will confront you.
   (To confront is to
   complement.)

I will invite change.
   (To change is to grow.)

4
Inviting Change:
Careful Confrontation

Life without confrontation is directionless, aimless, passive. When unchallenged, human beings tend to drift, to wander or to stagnate.

Confrontation is a gift.

Confrontation is a necessary stimulation to jog one out of mediocrity or to prod one back from extremes.

Confrontation is an art to be learned.

To affront is easy. Examples for being caustic, critical, cutting are available in abundance. "I don't need any lessons to learn how to tell people off. I do it in my sleep."

To confront is hard. Models for being candid, clear, confrontive without being uncaring are unusual if not truly rare. "I could use some help in learning how to confront in a way that doesn't frustrate or alienate."

The ability to offer another a maximum amount of information about their part in relationship with a minimum amount of threat to that relationship is a skill to be learned bit upon bit, new response added to old response.

Giving another feedback on how he or she is coming on can be surprisingly simple when it is offered in a context of caring, supportive acceptance; it can be astoundingly difficult when interpreted as insensitive, non-supportive rejection.

Hearing confrontation from another is no problem when one is certain that the other respects, values, cares in spite of all differences; but when respect is unclear and caring is unexpressed, one can feel fed up with another's feedback before it even begins.

Caring comes first, confrontation follows. A context of caring can be created when a person is truly *for* another, genuinely concerned *about* another, authentically related *to* another. The content of such caring is, however, not a blank check approval of the other. The core of true caring is a clear invitation to grow, to become what he or she truly is and can be, to move toward maturity. Accepting, appreciating, valuing another is an important part of relationship, but these attitudes may or may not be caring. The crucial element is—does it foster growth? Does it invite maturing? Does it set another more free to be?

A context of caring must come before confrontation.

A sense of support must be present before criticism.

An experience of empathy must precede evaluation.

A basis of trust must be laid before one risks advising.

A floor of affirmation must undergird any assertiveness.

A gift of understanding opens the way to disagreeing.

An awareness of love sets us free to level with each other.

Building solidarity in relationships with others—through caring, support, empathy, trust, affirmation, understanding and love—provides a foundation for the more powerful actions of confrontation, criticism, evaluation, counsel, assertiveness, disagreement and open leveling with each other.

Leading with power violates love. Leading with love

humanizes power. Power without love is ruthless. Love without power is helpless. Power grounded in and shaped by love strengthens both giver and receiver. Loving power is the heart of authentic relating.

"Is this guy going to talk forever?" you wonder as the committee meeting drags on past the normal adjournment time. The chairman has ignored three suggestions that you deal with the group's stated agenda and is going on and on with one of his personal concerns. If this were his first filibuster you might overlook it as you've done several times already.

You check your watch. "I'll sit this one out, you decide, and then find a good reason to drop this committee in the future."

Or you could plead ill, you *are* feeling sick of it all, excuse yourself and leave.

The impulse to be suddenly frank rises within you. "You've told us everything we didn't want to know about X and would not have asked. I move we adjourn," you're tempted to say, but you care a bit too much to put him down.

"I'm not sure I was aware how important this issue is to you," you say gently. "We are out of time this evening. I believe we could finish our work in the last ten minutes if we focus carefully. Let's give it a try."

Confrontation invites another to change but does not demand it. The confronter does not make the continuation of the friendship hang on a change of life in the confrontee. Acceptance of the other person is not connected to agreement or disagreement. Acceptance does not exclude differing; it frees us to differ more fully, frankly, effectively.

Wholesale approval of another suggests that one is either totally unconcerned or radically uninvolved with the other. Cheap approval can be lavished on anyone at any time to any extent. But caring requires that one get interested in the direction the other's life is taking and offer real immediate involvement.

If you love, you level. If you value another, you volunteer the truth.

Confrontation is not a matter of tact, diplomacy, and smoothness of tongue. It is basically simplicity of speech, empathy in attitude and honesty in response (to sum up the guidelines for giving effective feedback into one line).

The following skills for offering clear confrontation are given as basic guidelines. They are ways of practicing simplicity, honesty and empathy. To be free to value another equally as oneself, to seek to see from the other's point of view, is to offer confrontation in a way that is immediately useful without being stressful.

When confronting, focus your feedback *NOT on the actor BUT on the action.* Comment not on the person *but* on the behavior in question. To criticize the one behaving in a less than desirable way stimulates feelings of rejection. To critique the behavior affirms the other's freedom to change, encourages the person to disconnect from the behavior in question, and invites him to consider another option in future situations. "When someone criticizes people not present, as you were doing a moment ago, I get uptight. I'd encourage you to say what you have to say to the person."

When confronting, focus your feedback *NOT on your conclusions BUT on your observations.* Comment not on what you think, imagine or infer, *but* on what you have actually seen or heard. Statements of observation (fact) can be made only after observing, must be limited to what one has observed, and can be made only by the observer. Statements of inference (conclusions or rumor) can go beyond observation, can be made by anyone, anytime to anyone. These involve only degrees of probability, evoke immediate defensiveness in the receiver, and offer more confusion than clarifi-

cation even when the content is accurate. "You're not looking at me and not answering when I speak. Please give me
both attention and an answer."

When confronting, focus your feedback *NOT on judgments BUT on descriptions*. Comment not on how you would
label the other's behavior as nice or rude, right or wrong,
good or bad, *but* on clear accurate description in as neutral
language as possible. When a value judgment is received
there is a momentary break in contact. A slow motion replay
of a videotape will show that the recipient's eyes close at the
instant the loaded words are received, a frown creases the
forehead. For a moment communication is broken. Description offers no such effect. "I'm aware that you reply to my
requests for information with silence. Please tell me what this
means."

When confronting, focus your feedback *NOT on quality
BUT on quantity*. Comment not on the character, trait, or
classification (qualities) of the other person, *but* on the
amount of the feeling, expression or action (quantity). Use
adverbs (which tell how much) rather than adjectives (which
tell what kind of). Use terms denoting "more-or-less"
(quantity) rather than "either-or" categories (quality). "You
talked considerably more than others," not "You were a
loudmouth." "You have asked for and received more of my
time than any other student," not "You are clinging, dependent and always demanding time."

When confronting, focus your feedback *NOT on advice
and answers BUT on ideas, information and alternatives*.
Comment not with instructions on what to do with the data
you have to offer *but* with the data, the facts, the additional
options. To increase another's alternatives is to enrich
another. The more open possibilities available, the less likely
one is to move to a premature solution. "I've several other
options I want to report which you may have thought about,
but let me run them by once again."

When confronting, focus your feedback *NOT on the amount available within you as giver BUT on the amount useful to the receiver*. Comment not to ventilate and get release from your pent-up feelings *but* to give something of worth to the other, something helpful to another. Offer it, do not seek to force it on the other. Report what the receiver can best use rather than all you would like to say. If you overload the other's channels you only block, frustrate and may do more harm than good.

When confronting, focus feedback *NOT on the easiest time and place to suit your own schedule BUT on the best time and the optimal situation for the receiver*. We schedule all conflicts either by conscious choice or unconscious hunch. To choose time and place purposefully allows us to have the best interests of the other truly in the foreground. "I'd like a few minutes for conversation after dinner. Shall we go for a short walk?"

When confronting, focus feedback *NOT on "why" BUT on "what" and "how."* "Why" critiques values, motives, intents. "Why" sits in judgment. "What" and "how" relate to observable actions, behaviors, words and tone of voice. "Why" gets into trying to decipher cause and effect. "Why" starts with being historical and ends in becoming hysterical. "Here is where we are. Let's examine it. Now is when we are meeting, let's encounter each other."

To develop the ability to use eight out of eight in offering another confrontive feedback is not so hard as it may seem at first survey.

Focus on the action, on observations, on description, on quantity, on information, on alternatives, on the amount useful, on the best time and place, dealing with what and how in the here and now.

Do not focus on the actor, on conclusions, on judgments, on qualities, on advice, on the amount available, on the easiest time and place, or on why, why, why.

Simple, honest, empathic speech can achieve most of these positive goals, eliminate many of the pitfalls.

It's the end of a usual evening. You're stretched out in your favorite chair when your wife pulls up beside you, pad and pencil in hand.

"May I read you the collected sayings of Chairman You-know-who from the moment you got home until now?" (focus on behavior.)

"Yeah, if it's all that good," you say.

"Okay. 5:35, 'Hi, I'm home.' 6:20, 'Hamburger again? That all we can afford?' 7:14, 'How come the paper's wet?' 8:30, 'Switch the channel. That's a lousy show.' " (Clear reporting of observations.)

"Look," you say, "you wanted talk? Why didn't you marry a minister?"

"All I want is a little companionship," she says. "You walk in the door, say 'Hi,' then take a vow of silence." (Clear description.)

"No, you missed something," you reply. "I walk in, say 'Hi.' You give me that I'm-burned-up-that-you're-late-again look and I know that silence is my only safety, so I shut up."

"When you withdraw, I want some response out of you so I do a little prodding."

The honesty hits you. The two of you are saying the same thing. But each is saying the other starts it. Maybe it's one continuous cycle. I nag, you withdraw, I nag, you withdraw, I nag, you withdraw.

"Honey," you say, "who cares which came first—your prodding or my silence. We're stuck in this cycle. How can we break it?"

"I guess I could say something warm instead of digging at you."

"Okay, and I'll say what I really want instead of withdrawing."

Clear description of what is happening between two people can often clarify a confusing routine or blow the cover on an old game.

Clear observation of what we are doing to each other and how we are doing it can free us to see an old situation with new eyes.

Clear expression of what is thought and felt by each person can clear the air and free us both to zero in on what is needed for more harmonious relating.

Clear negotiation of what each wants of the relationship can correct past injustices and choose ways of responding to each other that are mutually satisfactory.

The central goal in all of these is to care, to manifest concern for the other and to deepen the involvement each has in the other.

Caring confrontation is characterized by this constant concern for the other's self-respect as well as for asserting one's own needs for greater respect. When the other's emotional safety and security are as important to me as my own, caring will be unquestionably present.

Out of both good and bad experiences ofgiving and receiving confrontation, I offer the following five guidelines.

Confront caringly. only after experiencing real care for the other; confront primarily to express real concern for another.

Confront gently. Do not offer more than the relationship can bear. Do not draw out more than you have put into the friendship.

Confront constructively. Take into consideration any possible interpretations of blaming, shaming, punishing. These are the negative side effects of most confrontation unless one's intentions are clearly expressed in credible ways.

Confront acceptantly. Respect the other's intentions as always good. For the average person, motives are inevitably mixed and the conscious intention is invariably good when rightly understood. Little is to be gained in impugning motives or evaluating another's hopes, wishes, goals.

Confront clearly: report what is fact (observation), what is feeling (emotion), what is hypothesis (conclusion). Sharpen your skills of differentiating between facts and their interpretations. Do not confuse them. Do not state an interpretation as though it were a fact.

But do confront. It is not a matter of "if" I can afford to be real with you, but "when."

To care is to be there for another. Care enough and you will confront.

For Further Experience

Your task is to mentally construct the five alternative responses to the following episode.

Case: For years you have been unable to say no to the heavy demands on your time from a charitable organization which you have gladly supported. Now the chairperson is calling on you again to attempt to pressure you into heading up the annual fund drive, even though this is one of your least favorite tasks. When you refuse, she only redoubles her efforts to persuade you. You feel like saying:

"How can you ask me to do this again after all the time I donated last year. Quit twisting my arm. Can't you be more considerate? I'm so tired of all this load of jobs, deadlines and obligations. Count me out, mark me off your list and get someone who has nothing better to do."

But you reflect a moment and try other options.

1. Confront caringly:

(Try: *I've been concerned about your organization as my last year's schedule will show. This year I'm guarding my time carefully and will not be available.*)

2. Confront gently:

(Try: *I do appreciate your thinking of me in choosing some-one for the assignment, however I'm reserving that block of time for myself and my family this year.*)

3. Confront constructively:

(Try: *I'm not available this year; I hope you have persons on your list who will be eager to help this year.*)

4. Confront acceptantly:

(Try: *I can hear how much you are needing volunteers this year. I won't be helping on this round. I hope you are able to gather a staff to help.*)

5. Confront clearly:

(Try: *I have already said no in four clear ways. I think I'm able to continue to do that under any persuasion or pres-sure. I can appreciate how much you want to find volun-teers, however I am not volunteering.*)

**To be trusted,
Trust.**

**If you wait until
trust is deserved,
you wait forever.**

Trust now.

**Someone is waiting
to trust in return.**

5
Giving Trust:

A Two-Way Venture of Faith

"Don't trust anyone over 30," it once was said by those who thought honesty ended at 29.

Then 20-year-olds began to discover how hard it was getting through to the 25s.

"Man, you just can't rap with them anymore," they complained. "We just don't read each other at all."

Then the 18-year-olds began to sense how far over the hill these guys were who had passed 20.

No sooner had the eighteeners pointed this out than they were deflated by the fifteeners. "Just because they can drive, they think they oughta be able to vote. They're too smart for no more than they know."

That's where the 12-year-olds chipped in. "Those teenagers are terrible," they said. "Have you ever tried talking to thirteeners? They say anybody that doesn't listen to them can lump it!"

The 10-year-olds wouldn't stand silent for that. "It's the 12-year-olds that are a bunch of spoiled brats; they're hardly out of diapers and they want to tell all kids how to do everything. You just can't trust them."

The 5-year-olds finally got in a word. "It's the first-graders that cause all the problems. Just because they've got an education and can read they think the world is their piece of cake."

The nursery school tykes find that trusting kindergarten kiddies is quite a challenge. And the toddlers in their terrible twos find the threes and fours less than trustworthy. And the one-year-olds are still working at achieving basic trust. So who's to be trusted?

Basic trust is the primal learning in the life of every child. Basic trust is the foundation for all subsequent learnings. And it remains the key, core, crucial emotion in all human relationships. Trust undergirds, interconnects, integrates, interrelates all the other emotions and affections.

Trust is the root emotion. In stress we fall back through the levels of fidelity, competence, adequacy, courage, initiative, autonomy, will, hope until we encounter the fundamental ground of our being: trust.

"I trust you." When I hear—or sense—that message from another person I feel loved, I feel accepted, I feel respected.

"I don't trust you." When I receive that message from someone important to me, I feel disliked, cut off, rejected.

If being trusted is that significant to our own sense of well-being and self-esteem, then a climate of trust is one of the most crucial elements in life, families and homes.

Trust—breathed in an atmosphere of love—nourishes life like oxygen. Distrust tightens the chest with anxiety, burns in the throat like smog, tears the eyes with its acidity, and poisons the whole person.

Test it for yourself. Close your eyes. Withdraw into yourself for a moment. Say, "No one trusts me. No one. I cannot be trusted. By anyone. I am rejected as untrustworthy.'' What do you feel? There's a narrowing of the chest, isn't there? A tightness in breathing. You want to draw in air but it comes hard. That's anxiety. That's how it feels when we are not trusted.

A breath of fresh trust can give a person enough life to go on for days. But deny a child—or a parent—or any person— of trust and he or she starves on the stale air of suspicion and rejection.

One cannot live without trust. Deprive another of it and he'll seek it elsewhere, getting it wherever he can find it. Or he may come to the point where he says, ''I trust no one. No one but me—myself.'' That too is death.

We need trust to be human. To refuse to trust is to do violence to human personhood.

Giving trust is the central task of parenting. To withhold it is to deprive an emerging person of the core need of its being. To withhold trust as a means of coercing conformity (which incidentally does not work no matter how commonly it is tried) is to say: ''Until you measure up to my demands I withhold the breath of life-nourishing trust from you. When you earn it again, when I decide you deserve it, I may give it back.''

Since trust is the primal familial emotion, we will explore it in this chapter primarily in the parent-parent and parent-child settings. Observations offered as to its nature are equally applicable elsewhere.

''They're a bunch of little devils,'' your husband says as your daughters back their love-bug out of the drive. ''Who knows what they're up to—sleeping around, popping pills, smoking pot. Either you're with me—and we crack down on them—or you're with them. . .''

You're in a real bind. You love your husband. You want to stay in touch with him. But you love your daughters too.

Nothing can persuade you to feel so coldly rejecting, so angrily judging as your husband wants you to be.

"I'm not going to reject either side," you tell yourself. "Both my husband and my daughters need me. I need them. I won't let his suspicions and anger stop me from giving trust to the girls, nor will I let myself be cut off from him. My daughters' problems are not going to come between us."

But what if a son—or a daughter—doesn't earn your trust? What if your trust is betrayed?

"I can't trust you anymore," parents often say. That's not true. The word "can't" is false. "I won't trust you anymore" would be a more honest statement.

"Can't" is an irresponsible word. It says, "Circumstances prevent me, others thwart me, you have stopped me. I am not responsible. I can do nothing." When you change the words "I can't" to "I won't" the truth begins to surface bringing responsibility with it.

When does a parent have the right to say, "I won't trust you anymore"? Only when they have come to the end of their parenting. When they choose to say, "Stop the family, I want to get off."

"You don't trust me anymore," children more often say to their parents. That's a line of many meanings.

It may say: "I'm confused. I've just betrayed my own ideals. I've done things I'm ashamed of. Tell me that you trust me. I need a breath of trust."

Or it may be saying: "I'm angry. You talk about responsibility. But when I want to make a decision you insist on making it for me. I need room to move, to breathe, to be me."

Or it can mean: "I'm frustrated. You use your trust to manipulate me. I feel your trust has many strings attached like, 'I'll trust you if. . .and only if. . .' But do you trust my ability to choose what seems right to me?"

Or it may mean: "I'm betrayed. You told me you trusted me so I made the decision that seemed important to me. Now

I see you don't respect me or my decision at all. Not at all. You bear-trapped me. You led me to think I was free to choose, then snap. I'm caught and rejected."

Or the phrase may communicate: "*I'm guilty.* I let you down. I admit it. I need my quota of mistakes. If you expect me to be perfect—according to your own standards—then 'trust' is the wrong word for our relationship. 'Obey' maybe, or 'copy.' But is that what you want—a rerun of your life?"

"You don't trust us anymore," your son says as you refuse him the car and demand that he and his brother cancel their plans for a weekend at the beach. He's right. You don't trust him, but you don't want to put it that boldly.

"Trust has got to be earned," you say to yourself. "If the guys want trust they'll have to prove themselves for the next month." But you know from experience that demanding trust be earned usually ends in mutual distrust and secrecy.

"I could say, 'Fellows, you want us to trust you to use your best judgment. Okay, we will. And we want you to trust us to use our best judgment in setting a few limits. . .' "

It's possible to affirm trust in your son even while rejecting untrustworthy acts. Saying, "I'm trusting you to try again—in a better way," opens the door to understanding. Trust is love that forgets the past, reaches out here and now to believe and encourage others, and gives them the freedom to claim the future.

What does a child mean when he/she says, "You don't trust me"? Perhaps it's simply, "You're cutting me off. Give me a second chance. Stay with me." Whatever the meaning, what can you answer?

You might try something like this:

"Yes, I trust you to use your best judgment. But I know from my own experience that one person's best judgment may not include quite enough important facts of knowledge to be completely dependable. And sometimes it may need buttressing with some help from others—even parents. If it's important to you that we trust you to use your best judgment, will you trust us to use our best judgment in the questions we raise and the suggestions we make?''

That's a long answer to be sure; but it can afford to be since trust goes both ways. And parents and children must constantly keep it alive and nourish it.

"So you don't want to be a doctor or teach. But isn't there some respectable occupation that appeals to you?" You stare at your silent son in total exasperation. "No, man," he says, "I think I'll just drift awhile and look at life. Then maybe find a little primitive land somewhere and go back to the soil. So you can keep your dreams of my future. I won't be needing them. Working and slaving for 40 years in the establishment only earns you ulcers and a taste for tranquilizers. Who needs all that capital to be happy? Who needs all that worry about Dow-Jones closings? I want to live.''

You hear his values. They're worlds apart from your own. Will you respect them? Or try to force him into some position where he has to yield to your values?

"Son," you say, "I want to be able to appreciate your values whether I share them or not. And you matter so much to me I want to know that you can see and respect my values too, even though you disagree with them. . . .''

To be trusted, you must trust. To receive trust from others, you risk trusting them by opening yourself to them. These two go together—trust and openness.

A climate of mutual trust develops out of mutual freedom to express real feelings, positive and negative. As each person moves toward a greater acceptance of his total self, more and more of his/her potential for loving, trusting, responsibility and growth are released.

And as the trust level rises the willingness to risk being open with each other increases too. The two go hand in hand. Trust and risk. Acceptance and honesty. Each is advanced by the other; each is dependent on the other; they are mutually strengthening.

There are risks involved in all love, acceptance, and trust. If I come to understand another's inner world, if I can sense his confusion or his timidity or his feeling of being treated unfairly, if I can feel it as if it were my own, then a highly sensitive empathy comes into play between us. A rare kind of trusting-understanding develops.

This is far different from the understanding which says: "I know what's wrong with you," or "I can see what makes you act that way."

This trusting-understanding enters the other's world in his or her own terms. And that is risky. If I take your world into mine, I run the risk of being changed, of becoming more like you.[5]

"You quit your job? But that's stupid," you snap at your son.

"You had a good thing going after school and now you drop it. You'll never amount to anything."

"Yeah, well, I just wasn't digging the work anymore. I decided to split," he says.

"At this rate," you say, "you'll never be worth a thing."

"If that's how you say it will be—that's how it will be."

He's shrugging you off coolly, turning away.

You're stuck at the usual impasse

You writing him off, he tuning you out.

You predicting failure, keeping score on his mistakes digging at past hurts to prod him along. He fighting back, spiting you at every chance.

Someone's got to break the cycle. Your worst predictions

keep coming true like prophecies that fulfill themselves.

"I've got to take the first step," you say. "The boy doesn't need me on his back. He needs me backing him up with trust and encouragement."

Trust is a two-way street. Two-way honesty. Trust, by its very nature, aims at interpersonal truth. Trusting another with the truth about me is the only authentic way of inviting the other to share the truth of his or her experience. Trusting follows truthing; truthing increases trusting.

The truth that is essential to trust relationships is grounded in authentic self-disclosure. "All truth is self-disclosure," so begins a major philosophic premise of contemporary thought. Truth is owning what is, recognizing what is given within us, affirming what is potential, actual and thus possible. Such truthing opens itself to another—vulnerably yet powerfully.

Trust with integrity is trust with its eyes open. Trust that cares enough to confront the other responsibly and with equal requests for the other to assume his or her responsibility to be equally honest, frank, out in the open with what he or she is choosing to do. Such trust willingly accepts apologies, forgives the past, cancels old debts, and gives the other his or her future back again.

For example, trust between intimates is based on *open love*—clear messages of affection and fidelity, and *open honesty*—clear statements of what I want, how I feel, how I behave and act in all my relationships.

Love and honesty are inseparable parts of trust because trust is a relational thing, a two-way experience.

It is circular.

Continuous.

Reciprocal.

It is trust—*between*.

It is the loving honest exchange of two or more persons as they interact and interrelate.

Trust is not a personal quality, a character trait, a Christian virtue to be possessed and prized. Trust is a relationship of risk and reliability, of honesty with loyalty, of goodness with genuineness. Trust is the basic stuff of all relationships.

For Further Experience
Trust is an attitude which, though not observable, can be inferred from certain actions we call "trust-behaviors." Check yourself. Which behaviors are characteristic of your relationships?

Distrust	*Trust*
Constantly evaluating others.	Avoiding all value judgments of persons and personalities.
Directing judgmental statements at persons and personalities.	Objecting to specific behaviors, not the "behaver"
Attempting to control another's actions, words, expression of feelings.	Respecting freedom to think, feel, choose.
Using strategies to get desired outcomes, manipulation or threat.	Making simple, honest statements and clear open requests.
Acting neutral when feelings get tense.	Being willing to give of yourself when there is risk.
Acting distant and superior when another feels weak or hurt.	Being vulnerable as an equal with equals.

Demanding
absolute promises and
ironclad guarantees from
others.

Dogmatically asserting
your opinions and view-
points as right and al-
ways right.

Allowing
room for spontaneous
choices, responses and
actions.

Giving
tentative statements
which are open to others'
feelings.

I
blame
you . . .

. . . and you
blame
me?

It's
all your
fault . . .

. . . it
started
with
me?

It's
your
move
first . . .

. . . it's
all
up to
me?

Let's . . . call
off
the
game.

6
Ending Blame:

Forget Whose Fault

I am always responsible for whatever I think, feel or do.

I am never to blame.

I am always accountable for whatever I choose or do not choose.

I am not available for shame.

Effective confrontation is sharply focused on responsibility. Expressed responsibly, addressed to responsibility.

Confrontation which places blame contains within itself the source of its own dysfunction. Blame inevitably evokes resistance and resentment whether conscious at the moment or later upon reflection and review.

Confrontation which probes for shame possesses within itself the guarantee of its own defeat. Shame invariably elicits self-doubt and depressive pain which then provoke new drives for expressing the original behavior again. The confrontation serves only to increase the actions it intended to eliminate.

Confrontation which stimulates responsibility invites the other to look at past behavior more objectively and to consider new behavior which can be more satisfying to both persons. Such feedback simply recognizes the time boundaries that exist. The past must be honored as past, the present seized, the future envisioned.

Responsibility is focused on the present and its openness to the future. Responsibility recognizes the ability to respond which is actual now and potential for what lies ahead. I will have ability to respond in the future; I have no ability to respond in the past. The past, being past, is not subject to change. I can change my present stance toward it and alter my future behavior from what I did in the past. These are present and future response-abilities.

Blame puts down the past as though that will help lift up better future options. (Instead, negative judgments and punitive actions toward one's past tends to boomerang. The negatively loaded behavior sticks in the memory and in times of frustration surfaces insistently.)

Shame puts down the self that acted in the past as though self-negations will create a positive self-image in the future. Two negations guarantee nothing except more negation.

Blame is powerless to effect change and growth.

Shame is powerless to evoke inner direction and new course corrections.

The capacity to choose creatively is increased as one takes responsibility for the past and affirms the ability to respond anew.

"I never liked that car—we shouldn't have bought it in the first place," your wife tells you. You're standing in the kitchen holding the crumpled chrome strip you just pulled loose from the smashed fender.

"Why didn't you tell me you scraped the side of the car?" you say low—and with overcontrolled tones.

"It's just the fender. I scratched it."

"Scratched it? Who did you hit? Did you get a ticket? Does he have insurance?"

"Slow down. It was nothing like that. I scraped a post coming out of the parking lot. No accident. No police. No problem."

"Except for our hundred-dollar deductible insurance."

"Hundred-dollar what?"

"Never mind. Where were you looking?"

"Straight ahead. We shouldn't have bought that car to begin with. You paid too much for it. You were taken in. It's never run right. But oh, no. You had to have it. Thought it was sharper looking than Bill's, so you paid through the nose. . ."

"Cut it out!" you bellow. "That's got nothing to do with this fender." You toss the chrome strip onto her white table-cloth. "We're talking about you trying to move a concrete abutment with a Corvette."

"You should be happy I wasn't hurt," she says. "If I had been run over by a truck, you'd come into the hospital and throw a greasy fender on my bed."

"Oh, for crying out loud, stick to the problem will you?"

"That is the problem," she says. "The problem is us. Not a piece of metal."

"The problem is I've got to pay for a smashed fender."

Nothing ends blaming games like the recognition that the blame must be scored 50-50.

Nothing settles old scores like the recognition that everything finally comes out even. That's how it is in any ongoing relationship. If there is blame to be fixed, it includes both persons involved.

It takes two people to have a problem. In a marriage, for

example, neither I nor you is the whole problem. "We" are our problems. The trouble is with "us."

Both people are involved in the hurt, the problem, the tragedy of a marriage in pain.

Blame is 50-50. In marriage, both people deserve each other. All tends to come out even in the end.

Example one: "He's the problem," the wife says. "I've given him the best 20 years of my life. I've cared for him in sickness and in health; I've borne him three children; I've never refused him anything. Now look. He betrays me with some little tramp. See how I was wronged?"

Good speech. Good case for scoring blame 90-10. Ninety for him—the villain; 10 for her—the virtuous wife. Agreed?

Highly unlikely. When you've heard them both, things even out. Once you see how righteous and superior she appears to him, the score comes nearer 50-50 again.

Example two: "It's all her fault that our son ran away," a husband says. "She nagged at him mercilessly. She criticized his choice of friends. She picked at his hair, his clothes, his way of speaking. She refused to accept the girl he was dating. So the boy left. She drove him away."

He makes a good case for scoring the tragedy 99-1. Ninety-nine points against her, one for his own responsibility.

But when you've heard both sides it evens out. In this case, the dad kept his distance from his wife since the boy was quite young. His cool withdrawal taught the boy how to reject and write his mother off. So the boy did in reality what his dad has been doing all along—withdrawing, rejecting, running away from relationship and intimacy.

"Trading for this car was your stupid idea," your wife says angrily. "Now we're stuck with the lemon."

"That's not true. We bought the one you wanted."

"We were taken. It's your fault."

You hit the starter one more time. It turns over but doesn't grab.

"You've been had," she says.

You give the ignition key another angry twist. If only it were her ear. She talks you into the car then blames you for buying it. Or did you buy the one she liked knowing you could blame her when something goes wrong? Either way, you're both being had in these no-win battles. Somebody's got to make a move for honesty.

"Jill," you say, "we're getting farther apart every time we fight. You're out to win by putting me down. I'm out to win by putting you down. We both lose. I don't care who wins. I just want to be close to you."

There's surprise all over her face.

"That's what I really want, too," she says.

Whose fault is it when things go wrong? That's the first question that arises in many human difficult moments. For those who prefer placing responsibility elsewhere, the question leads to a wild-goat chase for someone who can be scapegoated with the main load of blame. For those who prefer to sponge up the anger and store it away inside, the blame can be taken heroically upon themselves. "It's all my fault," they say, "I'm the total failure." And even more people do both. At one moment they blame themselves for the whole tragedy, at the next they take another swing at the scapegoat.

Blaming ourselves is useless, for a variety of reasons.

We usually blame ourselves for all the wrong reasons. (The crucial things that went wrong are not likely to occur to us alone.)

We're not qualified to sit in final judgment of our own lives. We so easily slip into either total rejection, "I'm no good at all, I don't deserve to live," or we excuse ourselves lightly, "So what, I'm only human." (To assume the right to sit in judgment over my motives, my past and my true condition, is to play God.)

I don't truly understand my past. I know that my memories are selective. I recall those things that fit with my self-image.

Friedrich Nietzsche, the German philosopher, put this pointedly, saying, "Pride and memory had an argument. Memory said, 'It happened thus and so!' Pride replied, 'Oh, but it couldn't have been like that!' and memory gave in."

So it is for us all. Memory gives in again and again. Most of the pictures we recall from our past have been retouched. Most of the scripts we can quote from old conversations have been edited for us by pride.

Memory is museum.

Room on room of memories are instantly available as one flashes through collections of choice recollections at will. Musing through your museum, note how selective the artifacts are. Are they art or fact? Did you create them to meet your needs or capture them to record reality?

Memory is mystery.

"I can see it now exactly as it happened," you may insist. But it isn't true. The best you can do is produce a biased series of fragments which serve to reassure you that things were as you wish they were. Or they may warn you to be sure they do not recur. The truth of your past is known only in part. Even to you. Especially to you.

Memory is myth.

Some people believe that memory is a camera. They assume past events are accurately recorded through an objective lens and preserved unretouched. We have no objective past. Our reflections are just that. My memories mirror me and my needs, my values, my dreams, my interpretation of my serial life experiences. Memory is not a telescope for looking at a sharply etched and permanent image. Memory is a kaleidoscope that re-views the past, rearranges its detail, reinterprets its meanings for the challenges of the moment. My story is my mythology of my life which guides the organization of my life. Memory is a compass that may repaint the scenes recalled, but still points toward integrity. Memory is a gyroscope that balances the self and maintains harmony and unity within.

Memory is my story.

Myth or mystery, it's still my story, and a story worth telling. Yes, it has been thoroughly edited by my pride. Memory reports what took place and pride rewrites the data before the conscience—the perfect scribe—can get at it. Yes, it has been recycled and the most recent forms may be made up of the original atoms but the anatomy has matured. Still, it's my story of who I am today, what I am becoming now, where I stand in this moment.

"Museum tours daily, 9-5."

Venture into your museum. Claim the rooms. The treasure is yours. Explore. The valuables are precious property. They are evidence that you have lived, risked, failed, learned from the pain, grown, celebrated, broken free.

There are a few rules in the museum.

Appreciate the collected objects of art. Don't abuse the privilege of visiting your past. Do not vandalize your valuables. Look at them in appropriate awe. Do not criticize them. Prize them.

Respect the recollected experiences. Use them for you, not against you. Learn from them how to choose more freely, how to live more fully, how to act more faithfully in the future.

Acquit the memories from any and all charges. To attempt to change the unchangeable (what is done is done) is useless. To try to reform what is formed (what was, is) is pointless.

Be humble enough to take pride in your past. Great or small, it's yours. Have the grace to be grateful for having lived. Accept the grace to own how you have lived. Absorb the grace that frees you to delight in what you have lived.

Going through our old memories to place blame is like hunting for a black bead in a dark room at midnight wearing heavy gloves and a blindfold.

I want to, rather simply, own my past with as few defenses as possible, and live now in the present before God and with my brothers and sisters.

Recognizing how unable I am to judge myself brings me to awareness of how unqualified I am to judge a sister or a brother. Since my vision is as impaired as though a beam of wood were protruding from my eye, I am poorly equipped to remove splinters from others, as Jesus put it unforgettably.

> Pass no judgment,
> And you will not be judged.
> For as you judge others,
> So you will yourselves be judged,
> And whatever measure you deal out to others
> Will be dealt back to you.
> Why do you look at the speck of sawdust in
> your brother's eye,
> With never a thought for the great plank in
> your own?
> Or how can you say to your brother,
> "Let me take the speck out of your eye,"
> When all the time there is that plank in your
> own?
> You hypocrite!
> First take the plank out of your own eye,
> And then you will see clearly
> To take the speck out of your brother's.
> Matthew 7:1-5, *NEB*.

Paul put it:

> Love keeps no score of wrongs;
> Does not gloat over other men's sins,
> But delights in the truth.
> There is nothing love cannot face;
> There is no limit to its faith, its hope,
>   and its endurance.
> 1 Corinthians 13:5-7, *NEB*.

Love ends the blaming games and gets on to the real questions: What is the loving, responsible, truly respectful thing to do now? Where do we go from here? When do we start? If not from here—where? If not now—when? Who—if not you and me?

Loving is owning responsibility, breaking the lead from the fine-line bookkeeping pencil, tearing up the scorecard, and beginning again. *Now.*

For Further Experience

1. Discuss a sensitive difference between you and a second party—family member, husband, wife, colleague—after covenanting the following ground rules:

(1) All language must be in present tense.

(2) All comments must be here and now.

(3) All statements must begin with "I feel. . ." (And give real feelings, not "I feel *that*. . ." which is a judgment, idea, or criticism masquerading in a feeling language).

(4) All blame statements are discarded as soon as either recognizes the finger being pointed.

Now move on up to an even more sensitive beef (or complaint). See if you can maintain clear, simple feeling-wanting statements.

2. Finish the following sentences for each other with at least three endings:

"I appreciate. . ."
"I want. . ."
"I need. . ."
"I demand. . ."
"I resent. . ."

Hear each other. Cancel old hidden demands. Drop blaming strategies and work toward what you truly want for yourself, for each other, for you both together.

Order.
Please rise.

The honorable
Everyman presiding.

You may be seated.

Case one.
Humanity vs. you.

How do you plead?
Guilty or not guilty?

7
Case Dismissed:
Reclaiming the Gavel

"What will people think?" you ask your daughter. "What will people say? That kind of thing just isn't done around here. Not by our kind of people. I don't want to hear about it."

You see frustration turning to anger in your daughter's eyes. She's up against the old wall "what will people think?"

You've been banging your head against that wall all your life. In every decision you first consider, "How will it look to others? What will it do to our family name?" How you feel or what you believe matters little when the final choice hangs on others' values.

"Is that what I want for my daughter?" you ask yourself. "Blind obedience to others' expectations? What has it done for me?

"Joanie," you say, "it doesn't matter that much what people will say. Let me hear what you want again. I don't think I was really listening."

Both giving and receiving of confrontation must occur in a context of good will. When one is consistently on trial, either feeling judged or acting as judge, all communication is contaminated by this imaginary game of legal charades.

Clear confrontation occurs as I am speaking to you as an equal. No "judgment" intended. Good judgment expressed and evoked in us both.

Confrontation can be clearly heard when one is no longer feeling automatically charged or guilty as charged.

"Wake up," your conscience commands. "It's time to be in court."

"Right, your honor," you reply. Your conscience sits as judge when you're alone. But once downstairs your husband, wife, mother, dad will join it on the bench. Then at work the boss will pick up the gavel. At lunch Charlie will preside while you tell him about last night's problem with the neighbor who backed over your son's bike. Then tonight at home your brother-in-law Pete ("They're coming over for supper, remember?") will be presiding behind the desk.

And you? You're in the docket. On trial. Permanently. One judge follows another. The evidence is heard. You testify—often against yourself. The sentence is passed— "guilty," or "not guilty." And your case is passed on to the next judge.

You know the feeling?

The feeling of being constantly on trial?

The feeling that life is not a stage—but a courtroom. That others have been appointed to judge. And you? You're the judged. Always on trial.

And you put yourself there on the stand, in the stocks, or at the gallows with the noose around your neck.

You are constantly making judicial appointments.

You are handing out gavels.

You are constantly on trial because you place yourself on trial.

Every day is your day in court.

Every man is your judge.

Every disapproval is a new ruling. Another sentence.

"Claiming love for yourself is the real secret," Dr. Frank Kimper counsels. "There was a time when—though I was loved, I did not have the courage to claim it. Depressed, lonely, I felt no one cared about me. It wasn't really true, but I lived as though it were; and as a result I was sick at heart and sick in body. I worked for praise, thinking that love had to be earned. I assumed that to be praised was to be loved and to be criticized was to be rejected. So I was always on trial."[6]

Few things are more painful than to be always on trial. You must constantly work for praise. Praise is a ruling in your favor. Enough praise might add up to an acquittal. And a little more than enough praise might even convince you that you're okay.

"To be praised is to be loved," you tell yourself. It's not true, of course. To be praised more often is to be manipulated. To be praised is often to be used. To be praised is often to be outsmarted, outmaneuvered, out-sweet-talked. But when you live to be praised, it doesn't matter. No price is too great for a little praise. "Just can't get enough of that praise!"

But when you get it, it's nothing. It turns to vapor in your grasp. You work for praise and approval, live for commendations and compliments, even sacrifice just for recognition and public notice. And what do you have to show for it? Emptiness. Loneliness. And little of the love you wanted so much.

Because the other side is there to haunt you. Criticism. And to be criticized is to be rejected. To be criticized is to lose approval, respect, love, and everything you're working toward.

That's not true either, of course. To be criticized is often to be truly appreciated. To be respected so much that the other person can share both positive and negative feelings about you. To be criticized by a real friend is to be loved.

But when you put yourself on trial, criticism is seen as rejection and praise is viewed as acceptance.

What a way to live! What a way to *not* live. To be constantly on trial is not living. It is existing as a shadow, a reflection of others' approval or disapproval.

It can all end whenever you want it to. No one is constantly on trial unless she or he chooses to be. If you live for another's praise or cringe rejected under another's criticism, you are choosing to be on trial. You volunteer to be victim.

To measure your own worth or to feel yourself a person of worth only when the respect is coming in, is giving others far too much power.

You are you. Claim yourself. Be who you are. You are a person of worth. Own yourself. Recognize what you are. Reclaim the power to be who you are in spite of your moment-to-moment performance, regardless of your day-to-day achievements. Be who you are before God and before others.

When you are permanently off trial, when your judges have been reclaimed as friends, equals, colleagues, you will notice a key difference begins to occur in most of your relationships. You no longer wield a gavel over others. When you are off trial, your friends, enemies, co-workers will be acquitted as well.

Think of those persons whose approval is all-important to you. Visualize them. Fantasize them seated behind a bench, gavel in hand, powdered wig in place. Do you see their approving or judging faces? Now—in your mind—go to each one of them. Say, "I have given you the power to try me, to sentence me, to reject me. When you reject me, I reject myself. When you approve of me, I approve of myself. My happiness, well-being, and self-respect depend on your approval.''

It sounds so powerless, so spineless to actually say those things aloud, doesn't it? But go ahead. Try it out. If you do not find it fits, you can discard it. Say to that face who is now frowning at you, "I reclaim my responsibility for me. I am no longer giving you the power to reject me and cut me off from love, joy, and happiness. I am re-owning myself.''

Now you're facing the real issue. Will you accept love from others without needing first to pay for it in advance? Without needing first to earn it—then receive it? Will you claim love for yourself? Will you bear to be loved—whether you feel you deserve it or not?

We're at a very crucial point here. Accepting love. For many it's unpalatable. Unacceptable. Love is only to be accepted in return for work well done. I've been there myself. Even when I was told I was loved whether my performance matched all expectations or not, I didn't believe it. I explained it away. When others affirmed me as someone who is loved, I rationalized it off. It only made matters worse to be loved.

Until I claimed it. Accepted it. Received it gratefully. No questions asked.

That's the real meaning of what the New Testament calls "grace." To be loved—and to need to accept that love—right at the point where we don't deserve it.

But God, rich in mercy, for the great love He bore us and the immense resources of His grace, and great kindness to us in Christ Jesus, made us His own. By His affection unearned you are forgiven. It is not your own doing. It is God's gift, not a reward for work done. There is nothing for anyone to boast of. (See Eph. 2:4-10.)

Do you respond to love like that? Do you say, "I am prized; I am a precious person; I am valued, loved, accepted, forgiven''? Then you are no longer on trial before God.

Will you step into the same kind of relationship with others? Accept the freedom of loving and being loved without feeling always in the docket, always self-conscious, always on trial.

"You mean I'm not on trial?"
"Only if you put yourself on the block."
"And I needn't fear you as my judge?"
"I don't want the job. Reclaim your power to be you. Affirm your freedom to be yourself. Your trial is over."

> *I like you as you are*
> *Exactly and precisely*
> *I think you turned out nicely.*[7]

This song lyric by the Reverend Fred Rogers is a favorite of the little people who watch his award-winning children's TV program, *Mister Rogers' Neighborhood*. It is his celebration of unearned love.

Perhaps you have moments when you become aware of how little you deserve the love, acceptance, respect, and personal appreciation you want—and need.

To know that you're rejectable, and sometimes to agree that you deserve rejection, hurts. And hurts where nothing much helps. It hurts because deep inside you fear that if the truth were known, if justice were done, if all scores were settled, you'd be lost.

That's the feeling. A feeling of great loss. Of loss of all that is most valuable, of yourself. "I" am lost. "I am rejected of God," you may feel. Right at this point, the best words you could hear would be:

You are accepted—as you are.

You are loved—for what you are.

You are respected—in spite of what you are not.

God appreciates you if you can receive it. He can and does say, "I love you, I accept you, you are loved." And He speaks such love, knowing exactly what—or whom—He is accepting. He understands the full cost of such an act. So when He says, "I like you as you are, exactly and precisely," He does it open-eyed. His love is not blind.

And yet, His love voluntarily blinds itself to the failures of our past. When He forgives and we accept that forgiveness by letting it become real in our own forgiving attitudes toward ourselves and our fellows, then the old situations become forgettable. He ignores them. They are forgotten.

To accept acceptance when we know we are unacceptable is for many an unbearable, impossible task.

To receive help and to need to admit that we cannot help ourselves is no easy thing. For many it's an unpalatable thing that they simply will not endure. So they must stay stuck with their feelings of rejection, hung up with the need to pay their own way, frozen at the one point of great opportunity. And there they stay. Stuck. Painful feeling. I once hung there myself.

No words effectively describe the sense of freedom that comes when you finally let go; no language expresses the experience of being accepted, of knowing that you are accepted, of accepting that acceptance.

To accept another's acceptance at the moment you see yourself as unacceptable, this is grace. And grace received is experienced as joy.

To give joy to another is to extend grace—love without conditions and limitations—to another. It is to admire, appreciate, and enjoy another without trying to change him or her by rejecting parts of that person as unacceptable or intolerable.

To enjoy another is like enjoying a sunset. You do not command, "Tone down the reds. Raise the lavenders. Stop! Too much yellow. A bit more blue, please." You are not in command. You are in awe. In respect. In appreciation. And to see another person unfold and to enjoy that unfolding—that is grace.

Joy happens when we can truly accept another—and are accepted. "What if I am unacceptable? What if I am rejected?" we wonder in fear. And, at the moment when rejection is expected, acceptance is discovered in the other's smile.

Joy is the result of truly loving and being loved by another—warts, faults, quirks and all. Have you not experienced it when a friend comes close enough to see faults and blemishes, as well as virtues and strengths, and still loves you? "He knows what I'm really like. She knows me for what I truly am. Yet I am loved."

Joy happens when we can truly hear another, and be truly heard. Have you not experienced joy when a friend shows caring in the only believable way—by hearing not just your words, but hearing you. And your heart wants to shout, "I've been heard. Someone else knows what it's like to be me." You feel it in the chest and around the eyes. It's a moistness. Like tears. Tears of joy.

Joy is the enjoyment of being enjoyed.

Grace is the acceptance of being accepted.

Love is seeing another as precious, just as you know yourself to be precious.

You're driving alone. The hours stretch long. You find yourself talking out loud, answering yourself, and then listening in surprise to your own wisdom. At times you feel so cut off, so lonely, so isolated from others. You don't feel understood. You hardly understand yourself. At those moments you sometimes see through the empty charades that fill so much of the time spent with others. And you want more. More than anything else, you want to accept and be accepted, respect and be respected, value and be valued by the people who matter in your life.

While you're talking out loud, try saying some of these

things to God. Put out your deepest feelings, searchings, the longings for what you value above all else. Describe the kind of love and acceptance you'd want from Him if He were here.

When it's all out, experience the silence, the openness, the release. Then listen. Feel. Reach out. You may now be in touch with what you've really been wanting all along. Know that you are loved. Accept the truth; you are accepted.

For Further Experience

1. Do you tend to feel judged and condemned when you hear how others see you, what they expect of you, and where they differ or disapprove? Go to that person in your imagination and say, "I hear your expectations. I am not responsible for them. I want to be who I am and still be in relationship with you. I am responsible for that."

2. Will you affirm—"When I have chosen to act according to my values . . .

"(1) I will not reject or regret my action merely because someone has passed judgment or volunteered criticism against it.

"(2) I will not disown, deny, or feel a need to make excuses or justify my behavior.

"(3) I will change my ways of behaving out of respect for others' feelings and rights, or because I am finding more satisfying ways of relating to others—but not out of fear of their judgment or censure."

3. Say these affirmations to someone you love:

(1) "I am equally precious, as you are precious. Our abilities may differ; our worth, never."

(2) "I no longer question my worth as a person even when I feel others may."

(3) "When you criticize me, I will see you as caring and confronting me. I want to hear the criticism and not feel attacked or rejected. When you praise me, I will say a simple, 'Thank you.' "

I would
change . . .   (if I
                    could)

I ought
to be
better . . .   (but I'm
                    not)

I should
be able to
move free . . .   (but I'm
                    helpless)

I wish
things were
different . . .   (but it's
                    hopeless)

What do
I really
want? . . .   (I can't say,
                    I'm too busy
                    playing
                    helpless and
                    hopeless)

I'm stuck.

8
Getting Unstuck:

Experiencing the Freedom to Change

It's 2 A.M. You're stark awake, lying in bed reliving the day's work. You give up trying to sleep, stick a leg out of bed. . .walk out to the living room. . .oooh. . .you kick a toe against a piece of furniture in the dark.

Then you stand, leaning against the windowsill, rubbing your foot, looking out at the lights of the city. So this is what you get. You drive yourself all day. Can't sleep nights. Is this all life has for you? Long days? And even longer nights? Where's the enjoyment, the sense of meaning you once felt? "God, there's got to be more to life than this senseless routine."

You stop suddenly, surprised to discover that you're praying. "I feel so—God, but I feel alone. If I could just talk this out with my wife, if I had just one friend who mirrored what I feel. . . .I need something, someone to talk with—Where do I start?"

Why confront when change occurs rarely and slowly if at all?

Why confront when people are largely the products of their pasts, when persons are the consequences of their early childhood development, when humans are basically conditioned by their social situation?

What's the point in confrontation if minimal change, growth, adaptation are to be expected from the adult human?

"You can't change human nature!" True? On the contrary, humans are the creatures with the gift of changing, growing, creating and recreating behaviors.

To learn is to change. To learn is integrative, not additive, so all real learning involves a change of one's core self. Change, and the ability to continue the change process, is at the center of our humanness, our aliveness, our uniqueness as children of God.

Focus your mind on one of your friends. Choose a friend whom you respect most. Someone who has gifts you admire, convictions you envy and the courage to live them now.

There. You have a face in mind.

Now let's imagine what that person might make of your life if he had the opportunity.

Are you ready for the fantasy?

It's morning. You've just pasted your toothbrush and begun a vigorous brushing when you catch sight of yourself in the mirror. It is not your familiar face that peers back, but your friend's. The toothbrush clatters into the basin. You stand, openmouthed in dazed unbelief. How often you've said, "I wish I were in his or her shoes for just one day, and he/she in mine. I'd like to see someone else face what I put up with every day."

Now it's happened. Somewhere, just now, another person is facing your face in the mirror, going down to eat your breakfast, driving your car to your job, interacting with your friends, living today with the results of your decisions made in a thousand yesterdays.

The best person you know has just moved into your life, where it is, as it is.

What changes will be made?

Will a fresh viewpoint make a real difference?

Will a new spirit of hope and optimism infect your job, your friends, your work?

Will the abandonment of worn-out habits of thought and action make a change in your life and the lives of your associates?

Will one day's practice of new behavior patterns really make a difference in the world you normally touch?

What are the differences? Are they differences you want now? Changes you need now?

What is stopping *you* from making those changes? How are you keeping yourself from being the different person your work needs, your world needs, you need?

How are you stopping yourself?

You are stopping yourself from becoming all you can be.

You are free to change if you choose. Change as a person, change in your power-to-live, change in claiming your potentials.

To say that change is improbable, impossible, to say, "I can't change," is to nurture the false fantasy that my life is controlled by fate. The script for such a life-style goes like this:

I had no voice in my birth.

I had no choice in my parents, my family, my community.

I grew up in a vise. I couldn't breathe, move, grow.

I had no say about anything.

I had to stay in line, no back talk, no negotiation.

By the time I was five, my personality was formed.

By the time I was a teenager, it was all decided.
I was determined, my character was set.
I never had a chance.
Not enough love, support, trust, faith.
Not the parenting, training, models for maturing.
Not a good education, choice of vocation.
Not one chance to change it.
Not a single opportunity to be different.
It's all in the stars/cards/genes/fates/script/conditioning.
I live with all the wrong breaks, no luck.
I'll die when my number comes up, and that's that.
I never had a chance.
I've no choice.
I can't help it.

A police car pulls up under the street light in front of the town hall-police station combination in a small Midwestern town. Two deputies pull a disheveled girl from the back seat. She flinches under their rough handling.

A crowd of men follow them into the office of the justice of the peace.

"We caught this hippie slut sleeping in a haystack with two long-haired apes. They got away. But she's gonna get it for all three of 'em."

"Whatta we do to her?" someone asks.

"Wait'll the J.P. gets here; we'll find out."

"The little tramp. She oughta be horsewhipped to an inch of her life. That usta be the law around here."

A man pushes through the crowd. He kneels beside the terrified, weeping girl.

"Have a little pity," he says gently, looking up at the hard, leering circle of faces.

"Okay, stranger," a deputy demands, "what do you say we do to her? We caught her in the hay with a couple of horny hippies. Don't you think she oughta have it beaten out of her?"

The man straightens up. "The one of you who is without fault, let him strike the first blow," he says evenly, looking from face to face.

An old man is first to leave. Then another. And others. The room empties. Only the man remains with the girl, still lying sobbing on the floor.

"Where are all your accusers?" the man asks. "Has no one struck you?"

"No, no one," she replies.

"I don't condemn you either," he says gently. "You may go. You're not stuck to the old script. You're free to live a new way. You don't need to repeat all this again." (Compare John 8:1-11.)

Can people change? Can life be different?

Wrong questions. Wrong words. Wrong viewpoint It's not "can we" but "will we."

Strength is available. Change is possible. Whenever a man or a woman accepts responsibility for where she or he is (that's often called confession) and chooses to make a change (that's often called repentance) and reaches out for the strength of God and the accepting love of some significant other persons (that's often called conversion), then change begins.

Yesterday I hurt a friend with quick words that cut too deeply. I am responsible for that. I am choosing to relate to that person in a more gentle way in the future. I am responsible for this new way of behavior. This is repentance.

I own responsibility for my part in what was unsatisfactory behavior. I accept responsibility for my part in what is and what will be new behavior.

Repentance is owning responsibility for what was, accepting responsibility for what is, and acting responsibly now.

Repentance is responsible action. It is not a matter of

punishing ourselves for past mistakes, hating ourselves for past failures, and depressing ourselves with feelings of worthlessness.

Repentance is becoming aware of where my responsibility begins and ends, and acting responsibly.

Repentance is finishing the unfinished business of my past and choosing to live in new ways that will not repeat old unsatisfactory situations.

"You didn't want me," the girl said to her mother. "You have never wanted me." For 14 years the girl has lived under the burden of a thoughtless word. "We weren't expecting twins so the second one came as a great shock." The mother's comment, overheard by the little girl at play, was her earliest memory. Feeling unwanted, she withdrew. The mother, not understanding, left her to her loneliness.

Now that she's aware, what's the mother to do? Punish herself for her lack of awareness? Hate herself for the damage done to a sensitive girl?

Neither would be helpful to either.

She can repent. Which is to own the responsibility for her part in neglecting and ignoring her daughter. And be responsible now. She can say, "I wanted you. You are precious. I want to be close to you now." And act responsibly now. She can plan new ways of being close, new times for listening and conversation, new ways of reaching out to say, "I care. Watch me. See how much I care."

I know a father who sat helpless while his sons were growing through their teenage years. "They won't obey me. There's nothing I can do. I'm a failure as a dad," he would say.

Meanwhile, the boys grew bitter at his lack of strength, his unwillingness to stand up to them, his softness when challenged.

What's the father to do?

He can repent. Which is to own his responsibility for copping out on his sons, recognize how he is avoiding all confrontation with them, and stand up alongside them.

He can care enough to confront them with his own strength. (He has strength enough. He's been using a lot of it to protect himself.) He can love them enough to let them test their budding strength against his, prove their decision-making ability by matching it with his.

This is repentance. Owning responsibility for what has been, wasting no time in self-punishment or self-hate, and getting on with the kind of behavioral changes that accept responsibility for what really is now, and what can be.

For example, you can say, "I was wrong. I made a mistake. I'm starting over." Or if your life-style has been a constant apology for living, you're free—in grace—not to apologize, to say, "I'm accepted. I'm all right now. It's okay to be me. I don't need to apologize for living. I'm loved."

The capacity to repent determines our capability to love and forgive and our ability to receive love and accept forgiveness. It is the growing person who can honestly say, "I have done wrong. I own it. It was my action. I am responsible for it. I am choosing to end that way of behaving. I am choosing to live in a new way."

The capacity to repent is directly related to our willingness to see. You've got to see how it really is before you can truly take repentant responsibility. It takes courage to see what truly is in our relationships. We are afraid and rightly so. Usually we are afraid for the wrong reason.

We tell ourselves, "If I let myself see what really is, all will collapse." It is not so. We can dare to see things as they are as far as we can be aware; and see we must. It's the only way to grow.

Our real fear could well be that things will not collapse, that things will not change, that we're likely to repeat the same errors over and over again, that, unless we own our mistakes responsibly and take responsibility to change, we'll be stuck forever where we are now.

"Somewhere along the way I missed it," you say. You're standing in the doorway to your son's room, looking at the empty bed. It's 2 A.M. God knows where he is. Or what he's up to now. "I don't know how or where it started, but I blew it as a dad. I really blew it."

You stand, head against the doorframe, going back through the past 17 years, wishing you'd done the other thing. Any other thing. And hurting. For your son and for yourself.

So here you are stewing in your own guilt over mistakes you made in parenting. When wrong and guilt and anger build to the breaking point, you take it out on your son again.

"What if I told him where I hurt instead of telling him what's wrong with him?" you ask yourself. "What if I told him that I care instead of cutting him down? I get in this cycle of—I feel guilty about my son—so I get angry at my son—so I feel guiltier and I get angrier. Admitting where I am could be at least a first step to freedom.

Repentance—in the full Christian meaning of the word— is a process. It's a thawing out of rigid life-styles into a flowing, moving, growing, repenting process.

Repentance is living in the open honesty called vulnerability. Repentance is growing in the decisive honesty we call responsibility. Both of these are processes. They continue as long as life continues.

To be a repenting person, I can choose to live in open, honest vulnerability before both God and community, and in clear, decisive responsibility to both God and community. This is repenting as a growing life-style. It is growth.

A word on vulnerability.

Vulnerability is letting repentance touch my defenses. If I need to admit to you that I make mistakes, I freeze. If I am about to be honest about my failures, my sudden fear is that I will lose your respect, your trust, perhaps your friendship. It's likely not true, of course, but my inner defenses keep telling me that it is so.

But repenting—honest owning of my own fears in voluntary vulnerability—creates trust, makes respect possible, and builds friendship.

(I speak not of self-depreciation done either in self-hate or false humility, but of simple owning of my own experience for what it is.)

Repentant vulnerability initiates, I discover, the most consistently beautiful and meaningful experiences in human relationships. People are lovable when vulnerable. People are believable when vulnerable.

People come to life as real, living, breathing, hurting, feeling, laughing, singing, growing beings when they are vulnerable.

But the price is practicing a life-style of repenting, not pretending. No person ever achieves safe-and-serene invulnerability. But we can pretend it. We can dream that it is possible, work to make it probable in our own lives, and carry on as if we are carrying it off.

But we never arrive. Our pronouncements continue to be questioned. Our pretenses are constantly suspect. Our claimed expertise is never beyond criticism.

We are vulnerable. We feel it even as we deny it.

We might as well affirm it. Own our vulnerability.

Vulnerability is letting repentance replace my old defense strategies with simple honesty, simple openness, simple willingness to change and grow.

Second, a word on responsibility.

Responsibility is letting repentance touch my decisions and turn my actions in new directions.

Repentance is responsible action. As I say this, I am aware that most persons hear the word "responsible" as a command, "You're responsible," made by some authority—either conscience within us or some controlling force without.

But the real meaning of the word is response-ability—the ability to respond. Persons with responsibility are persons in touch with their own ability to respond to others in free, vulnerable honesty.

I am finding that as I choose to be vulnerable to others in admitting who I am, where I've failed, how I hurt, and what I truly want in life, that the strength to respond in new ways—the response-ability—is there. Some of it is my own strength. Much more of it is the strength of God's Spirit within. (Who of us knows where the one ends and the other begins. We are only thankful that strength, courage, endurance, and patience are there. These are the abilities-to-respond.)

Repentance—open vulnerability, honest response-ability—is a continuous, ongoing process in Christian living. I want it to be at the center of my life-style. It's the key to growth, to relationship, to witness to God's work in human experience.

Repentance is hope. Hope that change is possible. Hope that I can be forgiven, loved, accepted by both God and my fellows if I only own what I've done and where I am. Hope that life can be new.

The capacity to see clearly where you are—
the responsibility to own fully what you've done—
the willingness to act decisively now in new ways—
the courage to follow through in new behavior—

this is repentance. Active (not passive). Acting (not just thinking, or feeling). Acts! (Not just good intentions or fine emotions.)

I've repenting to do, daily. I expect you may have a bit of it to do too.

I'm expecting it of myself. It's the natural order of things for the growing person. Owning what and where I've been, choosing what and where I shall be going.

Expect it of yourself. Plan it for yourself. Make it a normal part of living. Risk it. It's the key to life.

When Jesus came among us His first words were, "The kingdom of God is at hand" (the kingdom of right relationships is here). "Repent and believe the gospel" (turn, change, believe that you are free to love and be loved).

As Phillips translates these words, "The time has come at last—the kingdom of God has arrived. You must change your hearts and minds and believe the good news" (Mark 1:15, *Phillips*).

The wino looked up as he felt the hand on his shoulder. A dozen men had walked into his alley, stopped, circled around him.

"Sir," one said to the man who seemed to be in charge, "whose fault is it that this man is a wino? His own? Did his wife drive him to drink? Or was it his parents?"

"Forget the blaming games," the leader replied. "Ask instead, Where can he go? What can he do now?"

Reaching out, he put his fingers under the man's stubbly chin. Their eyes met, caught, held.

"Come on," he said, "you're free to leave skid row. Here's a five. Go on over to the Y, shed your rags, shower, shave, and go home."

Two hours later the man got off the bus in his old neighborhood.

"Hey, look. Isn't that Wino Willie?" an old neighbor asked.

"Can't be," another replied. "He's rotting in some alley by now."

"Sure looks like him."

"Yep," said Willie, "it's me!"

"What happened?"

"Dunno. This man says to me, 'Willie, you're free. Go on home. You're okay again!' I did. Here I am. I'm okay."

By this time a crowd had gathered. Family, old friends, two social workers, a probation officer, several local clergymen, a news reporter.

"What's going on?" they all asked. "What's with you?"

"Well, nine o'clock this morning I'm just sleeping off my hangover from last night's half gallon of muscatel, and I'm feeling like the DT's are coming back, when this guy and his friends come up the alley. He talked to me like I was people. Told me I'm okay. Said I was free to put the old life behind me. I could go. I did. Here I am."

"You're putting us on," someone yelled.

"Yeah, it's a hoax. You weren't really a wino. What's your angle?"

"No angle," the guy replied. "I've been splotched for years. Now I'm sober."

"Impossible," a clergyman snapped. "Once an alcoholic, always an alcoholic."

"Could be," the man replied. "This I do know. Once I was wet, now I'm dry."

"Tell us again what happened," the crowd demanded.

"Why? Are you open to changing too? You want to taste a little of this freedom to be different?"

"Change? Nothing doing! You can't change human nature. You're no different. Just wait and see. You're Wino Willie and you always will be! Get out. Go back where you came from."

The downtown bus pulled in. Willie shrugged his shoulders, got on.

Back on the city street, one block from the bus depot, Willie ran into the man and his group of friends.

"They say I'm no different, that I can't change," Willie said. "I guess they're right. There really isn't any hope."

"What do you think?" the man asked.

"Me? I dunno. But I felt today like I really am different, like God touched me, like I really can be free. Like it's okay to be me."

"That's all true. You can go on being free. And God is with you, see?"

"Yes, I think I see. But my family, my friends, why don't they see it?"

"None are so blind as those who will not see!" (Compare John 9:1-41.)

For Further Experience

1. When you feel you're up against a wall, and unable to change, consider Reinhold Niebuhr's classic prayer:

> God grant me the serenity
> To accept things I cannot change,
> Courage to change things I can,
> And the wisdom to know the difference.

Exercise that wisdom. Which things can you change? How? Here and now? Arrange them in two columns.

I cannot change	I can change
my age	my youthfulness
my sex	my awareness of sexuality
my family	my family relationships

2. In owning, repenting, and finishing past experiences affirm to yourself, to a significant other person, to God with this person that

(1) I do not deny the facts of my own past experiences, I do not need to overlook them, I will not distort and justify

them. They are past expressions of my freedom to be me. They are no longer me. I am forgiven. I am free.

(2) I here and now take responsibility for making my own decisions (I want information from others, I want understanding love from those near to me, I want to be aware of the way of Jesus), but I am fully responsible for my choices—satisfying or not—and I accept the consequences of my own behavior.

(3) I recognize and respond to "God at work within me—giving me both the will to do and the power to perform." I own and choose "to work out this salvation with a proper sense of awe and responsibility" (paraphrase of *Phillips'* version of Phil. 2:12,13).

I used to be a bit biased myself.
   (Now I have this thing
   about all biased people,
   they bug me.)

I used to be prejudiced myself.
   (Now I can't stand prejudiced
   people who can't accept
   others who differ from them.)

I used to hate the guys that smoke.
   (Now I hate the guys
   who hate the guys
   that smoke.)

9
Prejudice:

What Has It Done for You Lately?

"Talk about going after every cent you got," you say to the guys over lunch. "You gotta count your fingers to see if you've got 'em all when you leave the clothing store at the mall."

You grin appreciatively as the fellows chuckle. Then it hits you. That line was a direct quote from long ago by your dad. A rerun of his racial feelings.

"I don't dig replaying my dad's racist lines," you admit to yourself, "but it's a matter of habit. Those old family scripts get rerun in me like they were on tape. And I don't recognize the stale dialogue until I hear it out loud.

"I'm going to start listening for those old tapes," you decide. "When I hear them I can stop, even if it's in the middle of a line, and start over. I'm not stuck with the prejudiced attitudes I caught at home. I can choose my words. I can choose new ways of feeling toward people of different backgrounds."

Clear confrontation of another's prejudices requires that I be aware of, and wary of, my own.

Before I dare address another on his bias or her intolerance, I need to recognize my ever present tendencies to slant the issues, skew my conclusions, and shape my viewpoints in favor of my kind, my kin, etc.

I need to deal with my own prejudging—whether it be radical, liberal, conservative, or apathetic. I am all of these on different issues. I am in process of changing and being changed. I may be useful in challenging other's opinions.

Somewhere the ideas began—
that whites think they have divine rights,
that blacks are violent, power-driven,
that Indians are unimportant, dispensable,
that Mexicans are lazy, irresponsible,
that Polacks are stupid, slow-witted,
that Russians are malicious, dishonest,
that Italians are emotional.
Where did the ideas begin? I can't recall who first implanted the stereotypes in my mind. Can you identify how these and their many variants first came to you?

No matter how, where, when I learned them, if the stereotypes of prejudice are with me now, I am responsible. If they are still with you, you are responsible. Such ideas stay with us because we choose to keep them with us. We reindoctrinate ourselves with strange ideas such as, "Black people are biologically different from whites," or, "Minority people are shiftless, lazy, and not to be trusted."

To keep alive such assumptions as though they were facts, we simply keep repeating them, keep telling ourselves that they are true, keep slipping them into casual conversations:
   "Minority children seem to have lower IQs."
   "The Indian has contributed little to our world."

"The race problem in America is essentially a black problem."

"The race problem in Canada is an Indian problem."

The words are empty. We know it as we hear them. Yet the repetition serves to convince ourselves that our prejudices are still serviceable.

They aren't.

You met the Roberts at a neighbor's backyard barbecue. They are the first blacks you've known—on a personal, family, social basis. You enjoyed them. But you were uncomfortable. You caught yourself checking on how the man was looking at your wife. You felt anxious and distant.

So you're just becoming aware of how deep your prejudice runs? You do buy into the old stereotypes—like blacks are sexual athletes, they aren't safe around white women; they have no motivation to work; their fingers are long. "Where do all these old lines come from?" you wonder.

"From me," you admit. "They're part of my memory bank. I call them up. I reindoctrinate myself, reaffirm such ideas each time I think or mouth them. Maybe if I talked about my prejudices with the Roberts themselves, they could help me.

"Me? Receive help from them?" There's another old prejudice. "Yes. Why not?" you say.

Prejudice is any collection of negative feelings based on erroneous judgments which are not readily changed even in the face of data which disproves them.

Prejudice is any set of negative valuations based upon a faulty and inflexible generalization.

The process of forming these generalizations called prejudices flows as follows:

We categorize to maintain our sanity. Grouping things, thoughts, and people into classes is necessary in order to handle the complexity of our world. The trap lies in our tendency to exaggerate differences between groups on a particular characteristic and to minimize the differences within all groups.

We stereotype to maintain our equilibrium. It throws us off balance to constantly be observing differences, so we attribute certain traits to large human groups. Often these are images chosen to justify a negative feeling—fear, threat, inferiority. It is a head theory to support what the heart wants to make true.

We sanitize all incoming data to maintain purity of opinions. By being selective on what we expose ourselves to, we automatically limit our contacts and possibilities. By being selective with attention, we unconsciously exclude all incompatible data. By being selective in our recall, we drop out conflictual facts. So only supportive evidence is admitted and any contradiction is seen as an exception to the rule which goes to prove the rule.

So we discriminate in feeling, then in thought process, then in action. And the contradictions go unnoticed.

For example, the traits considered a virtue in the groups we like (because we are like them) are seen as a vice when observed in members of unlike groups. If one is a white-Anglo-Saxon protestant, he or she will admire Lincoln for being thrifty, hardworking, eager to learn, ambitious, successful. In a Jew, such traits would be called stingy, miserly, driven, uncharitable, etc.

What beliefs, attitudes, generalizations and stereotypes I carry with me into the next moment are my choice. What prejudices and biases I keep with me are my responsibility. I am free—if I'm willing to accept the freedom inherent in humanness—to leave the past and its self-serving opinions behind me.

I have racist attitudes. I don't like discovering them in myself, so I've become expert at hiding and denying them.

Now I know that freedom and healing come as I can own these attitudes, admit my inner confusion, confess my apathy, discard my myths, and make a change.

Life changes from moment to moment. I too can change, unless I choose to be stuck with or to stick by old, narrow, self-defeating ideas and ways of behaving. Healing can come as I become willing to risk the pain of letting go of what I've clung to. Or hung onto. Prejudice is a bulldog grip. It is clenched teeth. It is a spiteful bite that grips the past and its stale ideas as a protection against the present and its realities. It is hanging onto the imaginary security of fantasies that "me and my kind" are superior in some way.

Healing follows a willingness to risk seeing, admitting, smiling at and saying good-bye to old generalizations. Then healing, forgiveness, love, and reconciliation happen.

What is prejudice doing for you? What has it done for you lately?

Think "Chicano," what image do you have? Of a short, fat, chili-and-tortilla-eating, lazy, uneducated Mexican-American?

False. Chicanos do not breakfast on tacos and tamales. Chicanos are as concerned with life-work-education-community relationships as any other group. Chicanos have as much to contribute as any other ethnic group in America. We will all be made poorer if we refuse to receive it.

Think "Indian," what image do you have? Of a dependent, dishonest alcoholic, who lives on government money? That's untrue, unfair, and unfounded. Indians have made as great a contribution to our cultures as any group in Canada or the United States.

What are we doing with such prejudices? May I suggest we are excusing ourselves for (1) being unmoved by injustice done to others, (2) withdrawing from human need into indifferent safety, (3) enjoying our wealth without admitting that our gain often demands another's loss, (4) demanding government programs that profit our kind and class while depressing others. And that's only the beginning.

What have your prejudices done for you lately?

Excused indifference about the whites-only policy in your neighborhood, apartment building, business, or club?

Justified your doing business with restaurants, barber shops, motels, and recreational facilities that welcome only white-Anglo-Saxon-worthies?

Maintained your church as a lily-white organization supporting the status quo?

Bolstered sagging self-confidence by putting down those who are never present to defend themselves?

What function do prejudices perform for you? They serve some end or they would likely be dropped and forgotten. Become aware of what you're doing with your collection of racial labels and stereotypes. When you become aware—truly aware—of what you are doing and how you are doing it, you have a choice. You can choose to quit it. Or you can choose to excuse it and continue it.

Let your mind float freely for the next minute and fantasize with me—

It's morning. You're rubbing the sleep from your eyes after punching the alarm clock to silence when you notice your hands. They're brown. Not their natural tan but a deep dark brown. (Or if you're naturally black, imagine that the hands you hold in front of your eyes are suddenly white.)

You stumble out of bed and stand staring in dumb disbelief into the mirror. You're black. (White.) Overnight through some unexplainable freak act of fate you've become another, the other race.

The bacon-coffee smells of breakfast tell you that your wife (husband) is in the kitchen. What will she say or do as you enter? Will her eyes scream rejection? Will she recover with that phony smile (too wide, too long, too many teeth showing) that signals rejection while it speaks acceptance? The smile you've often given to people of other races?

The men in your car pool, they'll be stopping by for you in 30 minutes. What will they say? And at the office will there be a new distance separating you from your fellow workers? Will the job still be yours by tonight?

What of your friends? Will they be just as close as before? Your racist brother-in-law, how will you get along with him? And then there's your church, will you be welcome now? Or will the cold shoulder move you on to the side aisles and out of the door in a short time?

You look closely at yourself in the mirror. You've got to go out and face the world, but right now you're not happy about facing yourself, being the self you are becoming.

Do you find fantasies such as this distasteful? Threatening? Uncomfortable? Do you prefer to avoid discovery of things about yourself and your feelings toward other races?

To be able to see things from another's point of view is to be truly human, to be fully alive.

To be willing to see life from others' perspectives is to begin to understand them and to know yourself.

To be concerned about experiencing life from the vantage points—or disadvantage points—of other races and groups is to begin to awaken to life, to the world about you, to responsibility and to love.

Paul has some incisive words at this point. "Look to each other's interest and not merely to your own. . . .If. . .life in Christ yields anything to stir the heart, . . .any warmth of affection or compassion, . . .[try] thinking and feeling alike, with the same love for one another, the same turn of mind, and a common care for unity" (Phil 2:4, 1-3, *NEB*).

"Try on another's skin. Listen until you hear his or her point of view. Then get inside it. See how it fits for size. See how it feels to be there where he or she is. See what love is asking you to do.''

Hubert Schwartzentruber, a pastor in inner-city Saint Louis, speaks with a prophetic voice on linking Christian love and understanding to Christian action.

''The best gauge to determine what another's needs are is to take a look at what one's own needs are. I want to be free to make my decisions. If we then see someone else hindered from making free decisions, we must help to remove that which blocks decision-making and freedom for him.

''If I need a job, then my brother needs one too. . . .

''If I believe that my children need a good education, but many people through no fault of their own do not have my opportunities, then I have an obligation to help make quality education available for their children, too.

''If I have a need for a house for the safety of my family, then I must be concerned about the need of a man who, for a variety of reasons, does not have a safe place in which to house his family. . . .

''If it is for the welfare and the best interest of my family to have health care, then can I be a Christian without also doing something about the needs of those who have no way to obtain proper health care?''[8]

Seeing life from inside another's needs as well as my own can broaden concern and bring awareness of my responsibility to act. Feeling life from inside another's skin can shake me loose from complacent enjoyment of my good fortune and calloused indifference to others.

You're standing, stunned, hardly believing you've heard your daughter's words.

''Are you saying you love this— this—?'' You see in her eyes you'd best swallow the racial label.

''I'm not sure,'' she replies, ''but I think we're in love, perhaps enough to choose to marry.''

You, of all people, are suddenly at a loss for words. Of all the men (your kind of men) in this world, your daughter gets involved with this— What do you dare call him?—minority person.

"Would you want your daughter to marry one of them?" you've often asked as a trump question to silence all arguments about races getting close. Now you're facing it yourself. And all the old lines about mongrelizing the races seem useless and empty now that it's your daughter. You could tell her it's beneath her class, that it just isn't done by your kind, in your family. (Not that she'll really listen to all that.)

"No amount of arguments are going to make any difference," you admit to yourself. "Threats will only cut us off. She is her own person. She will need to make her decisions. It is her life."

Confronting deeply-believed, firmly-held, emotionally-rooted prejudices is a complex process of initiating change on several levels.

As a case in point, let's explore the strongly-held bias against marriages between people of different racial backgrounds which are often culturally based, religiously expressed, and emotionally argued. Let's look at the objections as presented and examine them on their own grounds.

Objection one: It's not biblical. Interracial marriage is forbidden by God. All through biblical history, beginning with Cain, God has followed a strict policy of segregation. He called His people the Jews out of other nations, prohibited intermarriage, kept them separate.

Even the most superficial study of the Bible will show that such separation was on religious grounds only. There is not the slightest hint that color, skin, hair, or shape of skull mattered at all. And the list of great men who married across national-racial lines include Abraham, Joseph, Moses, David, and Solomon. (If you are unclear on this, read Numbers 12, and note God's attitudes toward segregationists and critics of intermarriage.)

Did the New Testament oppose racial mixtures? "Yes," say some, quoting Paul, "He [God] made from one every nation of mankind to live on the face of the earth, having determined. . .the boundaries of their habitation" (Acts 17:26, *NASB*).

Perhaps you already noticed as I cited this much-quoted passage, that its real point is that "God has made from *one* every nation of mankind." We have a common Creator, a common ancestry, a common bloodstream, a common destiny.

Did Jesus and His disciples teach integration or practice mixing of races? Consider how Jesus refused to go along with the apartheid policies against Samaria, and how the apostles welcomed Gentiles and Africans, Jews and Arabs into the new fellowship. There were no first- and second-class citizens in the new church. (See Gal. 2 and Acts 15.)

There are no biblical arguments against intermarriage. Its message is that all who follow Christ become a new race—or better; that we move beyond all racial and national distinctions and become one new people—people of God who follow Jesus as Lord. Actually, the Christian faith has no view at all on the problem of race simply because from the Christian point of view there is no distinction between one man and another that allows one man to be set above another. All men are equal before God. In Christ there is neither Jew nor Greek. For those who follow Christ, race is a cultural matter of interest, but of no significance in value, no barrier to relationships, no block to total acceptance.

Objection two: It's not practical; it can't be successful. It's common sense to oppose interracial marriage on the grounds that there is too little in common. The customs, values, and interests are different—perhaps even the language—so the marriage can't succeed.

Evidence is to the contrary. Japanese-American marriages, with great cultural and linguistic differences, have a lower divorce rate than all-American marriages. A study by Thomas Monahan of 8,000 interracial marriages in Iowa from 1940 to 1967, shows that marriages between Negro men and white women are more stable than all-white marriages and twice as stable as all-black marriages. The same findings come from other studies.[9]

Objection three: It's biologically bad. Many whites oppose intermarriage because "racial mixture," they feel, "will lead to the degeneration of the white race."

Dr. Lowell Noble notes on this:

"History reveals that the white man, who seems to regard mongrelization as the worst evil, has in fact, already been responsible for mixing the races. His abuse of the Negro slave woman resulted in thousands of brown or light-skinned Negroes—or should we say dark whites. The logic runs something like this: If the white male is responsible for interracial offspring, no harm is done, since it is the inferior Negro race that is mixed. Such logic is clearly built on white racism."[10]

The biological facts are all to the opposite. Racial mixture neither damages nor improves the offspring.

Objection four: It's wrong for the children. They become outcasts. Others oppose interracial marriage because the children must suffer greater discrimination. It is not so. All research indicates that the children suffer no more discrimination than any other minority group.

Dr. James Carse, a historian of Christian faith, speaks to this point. "Children of such unions will surely experience considerable hardship and disadvantage, is the most commonly heard argument. The fact is, that the 'hardship and disadvantage' visited upon such children, arise not out of their 'mixed' parentage, but out of their being 'Negro.' Disadvantaged? Indeed, because in his most formative years he has before him the model of two persons who have made an ultimate commitment in the face of an issue that hatred has created, the 'interracial' child is privileged.''[11]

Having argued the issues raised in support of the racial bias on their own terms, the central concern comes clear.

The core is volitional. The core is the will. What a person wants, wills, values, chooses makes the decisive difference.

At the heart of living in unprejudiced patterns, there are central commitments, such as these:

1. Christians—who seriously try to follow Jesus daily in life—will refuse to make distinctions between one race or another, or to make decisions on the basis of one race being imagined as superior to another.

2. Those who follow Jesus point out dishonesty and discard dishonest beliefs as they discover them And there is no honest base—biblically, biologically, culturally, or statistically—for fighting or prohibiting interracial marriages.

3. Those who follow Jesus will question and challenge prejudices that separate people, and walls that create distrust between people.

Look at Jesus Christ.

He was born in the most rigidly ethnic culture of all time; born in a fiercely nationalistic nation; born in Galilee, the most bigoted backwoods of that nation; born into a family of snobbish royal lineage; born in a time when revolutionary fanaticism fired every heart with hatred for the Roman oppressors; born in a country practicing the apartheid of rigid segregation between Jews and Samaritans.

Jesus Christ was born in a world peopled with prejudiced, partisan, fanatical, intolerant, obstinate, opinionated, bigoted, dogmatic zealots—Roman, Samaritan, and Jewish. Yet He showed not a trace of it.

Read and reread the documents of His life. There is

absolutely nothing to indicate feelings of racial superiority, national prejudice, or personal discrimination.

Those who stand with Jesus Christ stand with all humanity. They discard prejudice whenever, however, and wherever they find it, confronting it in themselves first of all; then, and only then, in the world about them.

For Further Experience

1. Become aware of the prejudicial lines that you find running through your thoughts, or appearing in your conversations. Track down the old habit-recordings which play like taped messages from your past. You may not be able to erase these tapes, but you can pull the ear plug, hit the off-switch, refuse to listen.

2. Become aware of the uses of humor to support old my-race-is-better-than-yours feelings. If you find yourself telling Polack, Newfie, Jewish, Chinese, Negro, Indian jokes (name your favorites), try owning what you're doing then and there. Put your honest intentions into words.

3. To break free to venture trust, love, and understanding, consider:

(1) How am I stopping myself from seeing all persons, regardless of race, nationality, culture, as precious just as I am precious?

(2) How am I scaring myself from starting friendships, learning to appreciate the richness of differences, developing genuine empathy for others?

(3) How am I stuck in old prejudiced viewpoints that are unfaithful to the Jesus I want to follow daily in life?

(4) How am I blinding myself by selective exposure, selective attention, selective recall of data conflicting with my views.

(5) How can I move into more open relationships that invite others to confront me where I am scared, stuck, closed, blind?

Peacemaking Is

Care-fronting,
Truthing it,
Risking,
Growing,
Trusting,
Disagreeing,
Forgiving,
Challenging,
Accepting,
Demanding,
Canceling demands,
Owning responsibility,
Dropping blame,
Forgetting prejudice,
Acting in loving
Reconciling ways.

Making peace is the Jesus way.

10
Peacemaking:

Getting Together Again

Wanted:

Peacemakers.

Caring people who dare to be present with people when they are hurting and stand with people where they are hurting.

Peacemaking begins by truly being there for others.

It's much easier to avoid making contact with another's pain. All that's necessary is to quickly give advice. Tell him what to do with his troubles. Tell her where to go with her complaints. Get him off your back. Get her out of your hair.

It's so much easier to tell a fellowman what to do about his hurts than to stand with him in his pain.

It is much simpler to be a problem-solver for a sister than to share any part of her suffering.

Peacemaking is first being truly present with another.

Wanted:

Peacemakers.

Confronting people who are willing to help finish the old

business of the past and foster the freedom of persons to claim a future with the promise of becoming a new community.

Peacemaking proceeds by inviting the past to pass. And being present with another in the here and now.

Finish the past by dropping old demands, canceling old criticisms and prejudices. Accept the woman or man who is with you now.

We are all free to change, free to be new, now. Free to become who we can be. Change to new life is the natural order of things when God is at work among us. "Behold I make all things new." is His pledge. We need to go with—to flow with—His stream of life-changing growth.

Needed:
Peacemakers.

Caring, confronting, valuing people who have discovered long-range vision, long-term goals, a long view of human existence, principles that are more universally applicable.

Universal principles are values which prize the equal worth of all humans, promote the equal human rights of all humankind, seek after justice for all God's creation. Peacemakers who have caught a vision of a lasting peace commit themselves not only to short-term gains but also to long-term goals.

Immediate solutions have their place. They can reduce explosive tensions so that longer-range settlements can be negotiated.

Strategic solutions have their use. They can create a working agreement among parties that holds together until a more stable covenant can be made.

Temporary solutions are often the best we can achieve. In every state of concord lies the seeds of future conflict. In every state of conflict the crucial elements for creating peace lie hidden. The normal rhythm of life is concord-conflict-concord-conflict-concord. Thus all solutions are temporary, all agreements tentative. Everything we achieve will be surpassed.

Peacemakers who take the long view recognize that the values which shape their decisions must be lasting values, values which transcend not only one's own culture, race and nation but also one's own lifetime century, even millennium.

Nothing that is truly worth doing is ever completed in one generation's lifetime. Nothing that is truly worth attempting can be accomplished by one person without the help, support, guidance, wisdom of the community. Nothing that will be lasting, that will endure, makes complete sense in any immediate situation, in any given moment in history.

So peacemakers take a long view. They seek to set their consciences by those values that have depth in the history of humankind, that have breadth in their universal applicability, that have height in their accountability before God and all that is known through God's saving activity among His people.

So peacemakers are people of conscience. Not the narrow conscience of self-accusing, self-negating perfectionism, but the broad, deep, high and long-visioned conscience of internalized values, convictions and commitments. This can make them appear a bit out of step with the status quo. They may in fact seem alienated, but that alienation occurs because they refuse to accept the alienation of an alienated community which has come to accept its own alienation as natural, inevitable, and permanent.

"I'm never opening my mouth at work on how I feel about any political issues, or race troubles, or any of that," you tell your wife. "That bunch of bluenosed conservatives would pick me clean like a flock of vultures."

"You're going to just stay mum, eh?" she asks.

"Yeah, buy me a turtleneck; I'm keeping my head in."

"But what does it do to you inside to keep your honest feelings hidden?" your wife asks.

"I don't know," you say. "It does make me look like a different man than I really am. I've got to do better than that. I want to be able to put what I really feel on the line—and still stay in touch with the guys. Maybe that's the secret."

Following the conscience is a uniquely human gift. It is a capacity deserving our immediate respect. It dare not be automatically suspect. Conscience is not a faculty to be feared but a human quality to be prized and valued. In communities of outer-directed conformity, a conscience that varies from the mass mind will be feared as a dangerous force which may make a person an intolerable misfit, out of step with the rank and file and, since different, someone to be excluded.

Without conscientious wisdom, human beings become inhuman. Persons become unquestioning robots. And human community becomes a mass of pliable and pitiable puppets manipulated by the strings of any chance chain of command.

With a "conscientious *wisdom*," women and men become persons of integrity, sensitive to values, committed to truth.

"Conscientious wisdom" is the necessary quality. It is a conscience open to and committed to truth—a conscience informed by obedience to this knowledge.

It must be a "conscientious wisdom"—not blind obedience to conscience. A conscience unexamined, unexplored, untested by truth can be a dangerous, even a deadly guide. No man will kill you with less compunction than a man who kills in obedience to his conscience. But a "conscientious wisdom" is a conscience open to, instructed by, and committed to the highest truth man has found in all that is available to him.

True, there are risks to following conscience. But more

crimes have been committed in the name of duty and obedience to authority than in the name of conscience.

"Conscientious wisdom" is a love of truth. It is obedience to truth. It is a willingness to examine and test all truth, to sift from the good the better, from the better the best, from the best the ultimate.

"Conscientious wisdom" is a kind of courage. It is the courage to be a person. Courage to believe in values. Courage to see meaning in life. Courage to act with purpose. Courage to conform one's loyalties to one's true scale of priorities.

"Conscientious wisdom" always demands courage because following the conscience is a vulnerable act. It exposes a woman or a man to ridicule, to anger, to public rejection, to shame, to suffering, even to violence.

(Consider Martin Luther King, a man who acted in conscience, a man who died for conscience' sake. Three years before his death I heard him say to a network newscaster, "If I choose to go on living by my conscience, I may survive at the most for five more years. I could compromise my conscience and perhaps live to be 80. Either way I die. The one way I would simply postpone my burial.")

"Conscientious wisdom" may be an act of faith. The faith that your decision is the most responsible choice open to you. The faith that choosing the right thing is the best thing even though the cost seems staggering. The faith that time will vindicate the rightness of your act even though friends may condemn you now.

Let's apply this to a case in point. Violence, violent systems and violent war.

"That boy will be a CO only over my dead body," your husband says.

He's beginning to shout at you and you're only reporting what your son's letter said.

"No son of mine is going to be a—conscientious objector. If he doesn't want to volunteer, okay. But to declare himself a CO is senseless.''

"It's his decision, not yours," you say.

"So you're supporting the kid's yellow ideas," your husband snaps. "Or are they pink?"

All kinds of words rush to your tongue in defense of your son. You bite them back; your son doesn't need your protection. Not against his own father. All he needs is an honest—and caring—mother, and you can be both without letting this divide your marriage. "Dear, listen," you say. "I don't want this or anything else to come between us, understand?"

He nods.

"Let's stick to our own decisions and let our son make his. Neither of us agrees with all the choices he makes. We see this one from different sides, but that's okay."

"You want him to go yellow?" your husband asks.

"No, I want him to be a man, who's free to choose his own values and live them. It's not only his right, but it's his responsibility to make decisions by his own conscience."

As an experiment in conscientious care-fronting, let's look at the issue of participation in warfare.

If a war were declared unjust by your religious principles, by other persons of careful thought—would you fight in it?

For example. If you had been a 20-year-old male citizen of Germany in 1940, would you have obeyed orders to machine-gun Jewish mothers, daughters, and babies into a muddy trench grave? Or would you have fought in the Rhineland in unquestioning obedience if you saw your regime committing the mass murder of the Jewish race?

Would you refuse to fight an unjust war? If so, how do you go about determining whether the war is or is not unjust?

You can't use the 20-20 vision of historical hindsight. You won't likely have access to international opinion in order to shape your own in a time of national crisis.

When you come to the actual decision, the responsibility rests on you. On your conscience. On your best insight, your convictions, your principles, your sense of truth.

How, then, do people of good conscience go about deciding if a war is justifiable or not?

The first option: A Blank-Check Decision. Any war that my government declares or enters I must support, and anything my government asks I'm responsible to obey.

This option avoids all confrontation, by offering blanket obedience.

We are responsible to obey our government. But to obey it responsibly is one thing. To follow it blindly is another. To give the state a blank check, "I'll go anywhere, do anything to anyone in obedience to any command," is to cease being a moral being—a human being.

If you accept any justification for war, you will fight in any war—just or unjust, legal or criminal.

No, the blind obedience of a blank-check attitude just won't do for men of conscience.

A second option: The Holy War. Any war that defends our nation and its way of life is holy, right and good.

This option avoids real confrontation by dividing the world into the holy versus the unholy, so the decision is made by the definition given, and choice is eliminated.

Is any nation's way of life totally holy, right? Of course not. To give everything for one's country simply because it is one's country is absolute worship. Nationalism becomes religion. Patriotism turns into idolatry. It denies that there is a God in heaven whose truth is eternal and whose kingdom is above all. Such idolatry is neither moral nor rational.

Sometimes this argument is stated, "Any war that defends our Christian nation, or Christendom against communism, or Christians against paganism is automatically right." Muslims, Marxists, Maoists, and Christians have gone to battle to advance their causes. But to justify a war as a

"Christian crusade" is like talking of dry wetness or hot coldness. Jesus Christ never sanctioned war, never approved violence. His every word and action repudiated man's way of hate, murder, violence, and self-defense. He laid down His life for the sake of others. He did not take the sword even in self-defense.

Self-defense is no Christian virtue. If the survival of our culture or own own survival is our sole remaining purpose, we are not Christian. Survival is not a Christian virtue. Life is not to be maintained by any means. The ends do not justify the means.

The third option: A Just War. Through the centuries, men have agonized over the decisions of how certain acts of violence or warfare may be justified. When a conflict qualifies by certain criteria as justifiable, it has been called "a just war." (*Just* is short for *justifiable*. No war can be truly considered "just" to all involved.)

This option necessitates confrontation. It is truly a choice forced upon the just and the unjust.

The Greeks originated the concept. "A just war" was any war declared by the Greeks against the non-Greeks, the Barbarians. The Romans added the criteria that such a war must be (1) fought by soldiers not civilians, and (2) that it must be fought with just means for just causes. Christians (after Constantine baptized his entire army into the church in the year 300) adapted those criteria for themselves.

Today our standards for a just war have been set forth in our individual national constitutions, sharpened by the Geneva Conventions on warfare and canonized in the creeds of most major Christian denominations.

All agree on four major issues:

A just war must be (1) declared by a just authority, (2) fought for the one justifiable cause of establishing an orderly and just peace, (3) fought with justifiable proportionality between the amount of harm done and the benefits hoped for, and (4) fought by a just means, respecting noncombatants, and refusing inhumane weapons.

Do thoughtful Christians apply these principles when they are called up to fight? The record is not too good. When wars are being waged by other nations, men and women of conscience are seldom hesitant to apply the criteria. But when their own nation is involved, objectivity and motivation to think in clear moral terms tend to disappear.

If we are going to be human beings, to be responsible or—what is more—to be Christian, the alternatives are (1) either we can endure the agony of deciding on the justice or injustice of war, or (2) we can reject war.

For the first 200 years of the Christian faith, Christ's followers, like their Master, renounced the sword, rejected war and died refusing violence even in self-defense. By the year 400 Augustine was approving a "just war"; by the year 1000 "Christians" were fighting "holy" crusades; and by the twentieth century churches and Christians were accepting violence as long as it served to stop the Nazis, the Fascists, the communists. During the two World Wars, bishops blessed bayonets and bazookas on both sides.

History testifies to the difficulty of making this decision. Christian thinker John Howard Yoder asks, "Did any Christians [who held to a 'just war' doctrine] ever conclude, after their government had committed itself to war that the cause was unjustified and/or the means used were inappropriate and that therefore they should not serve? Such cases [prior to Vietnam] are few, or nonexistent."

Once war is declared the pressures to give blanket approval usually win out over any and all moral considerations. For pragmatic, expedient reasons we choose "to accommodate the integrity of love to the realities of life."

Christ Himself chose not to accommodate. He chose love as the final basis of action and acted consistently with that love. His associate, Peter, reports: "Indeed this is your calling. For Christ suffered for you and left you a personal example, so that you might follow in his footsteps. He was guilty of no sin nor of the slightest prevarication. Yet when he was insulted he offered no insult in return. When he suffered he made no threats of revenge. He simply committed his cause to the One who judges fairly" (1 pet. 2:21-23, *Phillips*).

"Yes, yes, well and good," many say in response to all this, "but I'm not Jesus. So He was absolutely sure of Himself, His principles, His position, His actions. But I can't be. So I accommodate and go to war. It stands to reason. It's just good sense!

Does it stand to reason? What about this argument that "Christ's demands are too absolute, too narrow, too single-minded to work in an imperfect world"?

Granted, all people and all human ways of life are imperfect. That's only another way of saying that we humans at our best are only relatively right. (That is not to say that right and wrong are relative.) It is the honest confession that no one of us has all the facts, all the insight, or possesses all truth.

But that is no argument against Christ's way of nonviolence. It's the very reverse.

If our best reasons and decisions are only partially or relatively good, then to take absolute and final actions—to snuff out lives with bombs, to napalm the earth bare of people, to exterminate one human or a whole city—all in pursuit of some imperfect relative good is irresponsible to Jesus Christ.

If you choose to fight in wars you consider just, or if you with me choose to reject all war as outside the will of God, come to your decision in clear open exercise of your conscience, weighing all truth available to you.

Anything less is being irresponsible to God, to humanity, to our nation, to our world, to our friends or to our enemies.

Obedience to conscience is the only true patriotism. Obedience to truth is the only true statesmanship.

"Happy are the peacemakers," Jesus once said, "because they are called God's sons."

Yes. They are. They are people who recognize the God of peace as their Father, the Prince of Peace as their leader, and the way of peacemaking as the only Christlike way of life.

Peacemakers risk stepping into moments of conflict to do curative peace work, to heal torn relationships, and even to do a bit of surgery where needed. And they're also concerned about preventive peacemaking. They look for building hostilities—and help to relieve them while they're still forming before they reach the explosive stage.

How do they do this preventive peacemaking?

By following the way of Jesus. In these specifics:

First, they look at people; not in evaluation of what they have been or have done but by what they are now. Jesus-people (peacemakers) look to see what that new thing is and what form it is taking.

As the Bible puts it: "The very spring of our actions is the love of Christ. . . . This means that our knowledge of men can no longer be based on their outward lives (indeed, even though we knew Christ as a man we do not know him like that any longer). For if a man is in Christ he becomes a new person altogether—the past is finished and gone, everything has become fresh and new" (2 Cor. 5:14,16,17, *Phillips*).

Secondly, peacemakers look for strengths in others and encourage them. They sense where there are gifts and talents lying dormant or ignored, and affirm them.

As the Bible says: "For just as you have many members in one physical body and those members differ in their functions, so we, though many in number, compose one body in Christ and are all members of one another. . . .

"Let us have no imitation Christian love. Let us have a

genuine hatred for evil and a real devotion to good. Let us have real warm affection for one another as between brothers, and a willingness to let the other man have the credit'' (Rom. 12:4,5,9,10, *Phillips*).

Look for opportunities of affirming, of encouraging, of helping release others to become all they can be in Christ.

Love is the important thing, not brilliant insight into persons and personalities.

Honesty is the indispensable thing, not attempting to avoid and gloss over the difficulty with a glaze of sweetness.

Love with honesty, caring with confronting, truthing it in love—these are the keys.

Concern for mutual fulfillment, joint opportunities for service and shared meaningful work is the real goal.

Peacemaking love works out the mathematics of justice.

Peacemaking love looks after each person's welfare and concerns.

Peacemaking love sees each person as precious simply because he is.

Love. The word falls short when we attempt to put all this freight within it. No one word is sufficient to state all that we mean. With one exception.

The biblical word for love, *agape* in the Greek, holds a rich constellation of meanings that sums up peacemaking love.

The biblical model for love, Jesus, gathers all these meanings into one exemplary life. He is the model for the biblical teachings on loving relationships.

Substitute the name ''Jesus'' for Paul's word ''love'' in his description of this just, caring concern and things come clear (see 1 Cor. 13).

''Jesus was patient, kind, never jealous, boastful or arrogant. He did not act unbecomingly, did not first seek His own interests, was not touchy; did not keep account of wrongs suffered nor gloat over the hardships of others. His greatest joy was seeing truth come to life. He accepted all that people said or did to Him, trusted all who approached Him, believed the best for all who despaired. He set no limits for what He could endure. His concern, respect, and compassion could outlast anything."

That fleshes out the word love. The apostle Paul had an unusual word available to him to sum all this meaning into verbal shorthand, *agape*.

Agape has been defined as "benevolent love," or "self-sacrificial love," or "disinterested love," or "self-giving love," or "unconditional-concerned-respect," or "neighbor-regarding-love." The best definition that brings together the whole of biblical teaching on love is "equal regard." Valuing neighbor as self; prizing others as you prize yourself; seeing another as precious, worthful and irreducibly valuable is equal regard. These are action words, behavioral terms. Love is something you do. That's where our Western languages and Western ways of thinking shortchange us. For us, love is largely a matter of feelings, attitudes, and emotional responses. *Agape* is action. It is equal regard acted upon in equal respect. It's a caring way of responding to people as persons of value. It's a confronting way of relating to people as individuals of infinite worth in God's sight, and therefore in your own.

Jesus valued the needs of the neighbor above all else. For Him, concern for others is the supreme value, the one thing of infinite worth.

To be specific, to say that neighbor-love is infinitely superior in value to human knowledge is to say that no gain in human knowledge is worth even the smallest loss of neighbor-love. Or to say that neighbor-love is infinitely superior to any human achievements is to say that no amount of increase in human achievement and success is worth even the smallest decrease in Christlike love.

The Jesus way of love-in-actions-of-ultimate-concern-for-others is the one course of action which is of infinite value.

The Jesus way of loving-deeds is a life-style of living *for,* unshakably *for,* unconditionally *for,* unreservedly *for* the highest good *for* others. (Not in servile obedience to human whims but in concerned commitment to the highest good for others.)

Persons matter most.

Those who live in the Jesus-way of love seek the highest good they can find (God's kingly rule) and share it in acted-out deeds of loving service, concern, respect, and even self-sacrifice.

People matter most.

They act in love, not because it is the safe thing to do. (It doesn't guarantee either success or survival.) Nor because it is the brilliant thing to do. (It seldom is the clever strategy or the pragmatic route of common sense.) They act in love because it is the Jesus thing to do, the Jesus way to live, the Jesus kind of loving.

And since He alone has triumphed in the one permanent victory of all time—love acted out on a cross—His way is the only way that is certain to triumph totally, finally, ultimately, eternally.

So, for those who have come to accept this Jesus as Supreme Commander of creation and to regard His words and His ways as the final authority on life and living, for such people this strange quality of love keeps cropping out.

At unusual times, in unexpected ways, with unexplainable strength, this undefinable "something" appears.

It's the Jesus way of living, flawlessly demonstrated in the Jesus of the New Testament and made possible today by the Jesus strength-to-love which Christians call the Holy Spirit.

It is caring in full valuation of another.

It is confronting without violation of the other.

It is care-fronting in equal regard.

For Further Experience

1. Examine the four classic alternatives for the Christian conscience and participation in warfare. List benefits and liabilities of each. Affirm your own criteria for decision-making.

(1) *The blank-check approach.* Whatever my government asks, I must do. The Bible commands obedience. I am not morally responsible for any acts done when under orders. (Nuremberg, Tokyo, the My Lai trials all say otherwise.)

(2) *The holy-war stance.* Any war that defends a Christian nation or Christendom against communism is a crusade for liberty, justice, and righteousness. (Christians believed this in the Middle Ages. It has had no continuing support by any Christian group except in times of great national stress.)

(3) *The just-war conviction.* A war can be justified if (a) declared by just authority, (b) fought to bring a just and orderly peace, (c) fought with clear proportionality between amount of harm and benefits hoped for, (d) fought by just means, by combatants only, without inhumane weapons.

(4) *Nonviolent love.* War only creates the conditions for further wars. Violence breeds new and more vicious violent reprisals. Someone must break the cycle. Jesus called His followers to accept this challenge unconditionally. (Refusing to participate in violence is risky. There is no guarantee of either survival or success.)

Concluding Exercise

Choose a friend, partner, associate and test out the following assumptions as applied to your relationship.

Work through the differences that arise.

Reflect on what you are learning about life together.

1. If conflict is natural, neutral, and potentially creative, as well as possibly destructive, how can Christians best fulfill their roles as peacemakers?

(1) By avoiding conflict?

(2) By denouncing conflict?

(3) Or by becoming creative persons who choose the love-fight and break through barriers by caring-confronting persistence?

2. If conflict can become a creative force for honest intimacy, how do we work at differences?

(1) Discarding hidden strategies so that varied views and concealed disagreements can be exposed?

(2) Increasing both trust and risk so that hidden factors can be shared and fearful people can experiment with openness?

(3) Initiating love-truth, care-confront conversations where individuality can be expressed and then unity chosen and celebrated?

3. Since love is *the way* to perceive you as well as me, I want to love you enough to tell you the truth, and be truthful enough to demonstrate my love. To care-front. To truth it with you. To experience the love-fight.

Notes

1. John Powell, *Why Am I Afraid to Tell You Who I Am?* (Los Angeles: Argus Communications, 1969).

2. Frank Kimper, "Love and Anger," unpublished manuscript (Claremont, CA: School of Theology, 1971). Used by permission.

3. Harry Stack Sullivan, *The Psychiatric Interview* (New York: W.W. Norton, 1954), pp. 218,219.

4. *Ibid*, p. 109.

5. Carl R. Rogers and Barry Stevens, *Person to Person: The Problem of Being Human* (New York: Dell Publishing Co., Inc.) pp. 92-94.

6. Frank W. Kimper, *Meditations for Churchmen in the 70's*, 2nd ed. (Claremont, CA: School of Theology, 1971).

7. Josie Carey and Fred Rogers, "I Like You As You Are." Copyright 1959 Vernon Music Corporation. International copyright secured. All rights reserved. Used by permission of the copyright owner.

8. Hubert Schwartzentruber, *Probe*, James Fairfield, ed. (Scottdale, PA: Herald Press, 1972), pp. 80,81.

9. Lowell Noble, "What's Behind Our Interracial Marriage Taboos?" *Eternity*, July 1972, p. 13.

10. *Ibid*.

11. James P. Carse, "Interracial Marriage: A Christian View," *The Christian Century*, June 14, 1967, p. 782.

Notes

Notes

Notes

Notes

Notes

Notes

Notes

Notes

Notes

Notes

Notes